THE ANCIENT GREEKS

Published in 1996 by
Marshall Cavendish Corporation
99 White Plains Road
Tarrytown, NY 10591-9001
U.S.A.

Editor: Henk Dijkstra
Executive Editor: Paulien Retèl
Revision Editor: Frits Naerebout
Art Director: Henk Oostenrijk, Studio 87, Utrecht, The Netherlands
Index Editors: Schuurmans & Jonkers, Leiden, The Netherlands
Preface: Eva von Dassow, Ph.D., Skirball Department of Hebrew and Judaic Studies,
New York University, New York City

History of the Ancient & Medieval World is a completely revised and
updated edition of *The Adventure of Mankind.*
© 1996 Marshall Cavendish Corporation and
HD Communication Consultants BV, Hilversum,
The Netherlands

Library of Congress Cataloging-in-Publication Date

History of the ancient and medieval world / edited by Henk Dijkstra.
p. cm.
Completely rev. and updated ed. of: The Adventure of mankind (second edition 1995).
Contents:—v.4. The Ancient Greeks.
ISBN 0-7614-0355-8 (v.4).—ISBN 0-7614-0351-5 (lib.bdg.:set)
1. History, Ancient—Juvenile literature. 2. Middle Ages—History—Juvenile literature. I. Dijkstra, Henk. II Title: Adventure of mankind.
D117.H57 1996
930—dc20/95-35715

History of the
Ancient & Medieval World

Volume 4

The Ancient Greeks

Marshall Cavendish
New York   Toronto   Sydney

The Ancient Greeks

Attic red-figure pottery with a scene of a *gynaeceum* or woman's quarters

CONTENTS

Preface

The Ancient Greeks covers the history and culture of Greece from the Dark Age (ca. 1050–750 BC) through the early Classical period in the mid-fifth century BC. The volume opens with a discussion of the *Iliad* and the *Odyssey*, addressing the issues of authorship and historicity relating to Homer and the Homeric epics; the society of Dark Age Greece, as reflected in these epics, is contrasted with earlier Mycenaean society. During the Dark Age, the migrations of the Dorians, Aeolians, and Ionians altered the ethnic geography of Greece and brought extensive Greek settlement to the coast of Asia Minor. The succeeding Archaic period (ca. 750–500 BC) is characterized by colonial expansion on the part of the emerging Greek city-states. Trading settlements and colonies were established throughout much of the Mediterranean region and on the shores of the Black Sea. A concomitant feature of Archaic Greek culture was the absorption of Near Eastern and Egyptian influences, observable in the arts, in religious beliefs, and most significantly, in the adoption of the Phoenician alphabet.

The Archaic period was also a time of political development, as the focal point of social organization gradually shifted from local aristocracies to the city-state, the *polis*, governed through a council and an assembly of free citizens. The two city-states about which we have the most information are Sparta, with its notoriously rigid social system, whose economy depended on the exploitation of a subject population (the *helots*); and Athens, where, though great inequalities in wealth persisted, Solon's reforms helped to assure that members of all four classes of citizens would enjoy the right of political participation. Tyrants arose in several Greek city-states, for instance, Corinth and Athens; the emergence of tyranny inadvertently promoted democratic developments in some cases. Toward the end of the sixth century, following the downfall of the Peisistratid tyranny, the aristocrat Cleisthenes reorganized the governing institutions of Athens in favor of the *démos*, the "people."

The Persian Wars, opening the Classical period, catalyzed the emergence of a Greek national consciousness. Athens and Sparta cooperated in leading a coalition of Greek city-states to victory over the invading forces deployed by the Persian Empire. Athenians in particular used the opportunity provided by their newfound leadership to expand their city's international role and enhance its status as a cultural center. Thus Athens acquired hegemony over much of the Greek world by the mid-fifth century. Under the leadership of the statesman and general Pericles, Athenian democracy also achieved its high point during this period, with which this volume concludes.

Besides political history, the topics treated here include literature, theater, religion, philosophy, and science. Greek religion combined an Indo-European heritage with indigenous (pre-Greek) elements and influences from the Near East and elsewhere. The intellectual expansion that accompanied the phase of colonial expansion and Orientalization in the Archaic period led to new literary forms, exemplified by the lyric and elegiac poets, and of new ways of thinking about the natural world, exemplified by the Ionian philosophers of the sixth century BC. These developments culminated in the flourishing of Greek drama and rational philosophy in the fifth century, along with other genres of prose composition and the plastic arts. Extensive quotations from ancient authors, from tragedians to historians, illustrate the discussion throughout.

Eva von Dassow, Ph.D.,
Skirball Department of Hebrew
and Judaic Studies, New York
University, New York City

After Achilles's death, Ajax and Odysseus fight about his weapons. Detail of a Greek drinking cup, dating from the fifth century BC

The *Iliad* and the *Odyssey*

The "Homeric Question"

The literary history of Europe began with two Greek epics, the *Iliad* and the *Odyssey*, written, according to the Greeks and literary tradition, by a poet named Homer. Nothing is really known about him, even the actuality of his existence. The late-nineteenth-century discoveries of Heinrich Schliemann in Greece and Turkey and those of other archaeologists since lend credence to the historical reality of the Asia Minor civilization of Homer. It is now assumed that the Homeric poems date from the late eighth century BC.

Epic poems, including the forerunners of

Homer's work, were passed on orally long before they were written down. Text originally played no part in the *Iliad* and the *Odyssey*. Professional singers recited ancient poetry by heart or improvised on existing themes. In the eighth or seventh century BC, these oral narratives were written down in a form differing only slightly from the text that exists today. In subsequent centuries, the epics spread throughout the region, influenced by Greek civilization and considered Greek national poetry. The versions we know were created through the comparison of various manuscripts in the second century BC. The text, like most classical works, was repeatedly copied, preserving it for posterity.

The role of a man called Homer in this process is debatable. There is question not only as to his existence but as to the authenticity of his authorship of all the pieces attributed to him. Besides the *Iliad* and the *Odyssey*, these included several other heroic poems (called the Homeric cycle) and the *Homeric Hymns*, short poems in celebration of the gods. Various theories have been expounded since the eighteenth century. One suggested that the *Iliad* and the *Odyssey* originated from collections of short pieces, independently written by unknown national poets at different times, combined by a committee in sixth-century Athens. Another theory postulated that the epics were written by Homer, but as relatively short poems later supplemented by various singers until it was no longer clear exactly which parts had been contributed by whom. A third suggestion,

Bust of Homer,
made around 200 BC

After Hector has been killed, King Priam goes to Achilles to ask him for the body of his son. Achilles receives him lying on a decorated bed—the dead prince has been put on the floor underneath. Attic *skyphos* (beaker) from the fifth century BC

440

most popular today, is that the *Iliad* and the *Odyssey* were compiled by one or, more probably, two brilliant poets, who put together a number of coherent tales from fragmented oral recitals. Perhaps one of these poets was a blind beggar bard from Chios, mentioned in old records of the era, and perhaps he was named Homer.

Epic Style

In any case, the high literary quality of the work is undisputed. Both epics are written in formal verse, using dactylic hexameter. This meter uses one accented syllable followed by two unaccented in each metrical foot except the last, which is called a *trochee*: one accented and one unaccented syllable. There are six metrical feet to each line.

The *Iliad*

The background to the *Iliad* is the siege of Troy, a city in Asia Minor near the entrance to the Dardanelles. The besiegers are a coalition of Greeks, called Achaeans in the poem. The reason for the war is the abduction of the beautiful Helen, wife of Menelaus, king of Sparta, by a Trojan prince named Paris. Menelaus and his brother Agamemnon, king of Mycenae, call upon the princes of Achaea to punish Troy and bring Helen home. A fleet is prepared and sails for Troy, where a long, drawn-out siege follows.

At Troy, a dispute arises between the Greek prince Achilles and the supreme commander Agamemnon, who abuses his authority by taking a beautiful slave away from Achilles. This slave had been given to Achilles as a prize of war. Achilles is deeply insulted by Agamemnon's behavior. Achilles subsequently refuses to continue fighting on the side of the Achaeans and sits sulking in his tent.

Without Achilles, the Greeks prove to be weaker than the Trojans, who are led by Hector. Disaster threatens. Achilles finally agrees to allow his friend Patroclus to take part in the conflict. Patroclus is killed by Hector. The grieving Achilles feels compelled to avenge his friend and subsequently kills Hector, which heralds the beginning of the end for the Trojans. The *Iliad* ends with the burial of Patroclus and the return of Hector's body to his father, King Priam. The entire episode covers only a brief interlude of fifty-one days in the ten-year Trojan War, although an impression is given of the war as a whole by means of allusion. All of the characters are simply caught up in a tragic sequence of passions and events.

The *Odyssey*

The *Odyssey* is a kind of sequel, dealing with

The conquest of Troy by the Greeks, as painted on an Attic *kalpis* (water pitcher) made in the fifth century BC

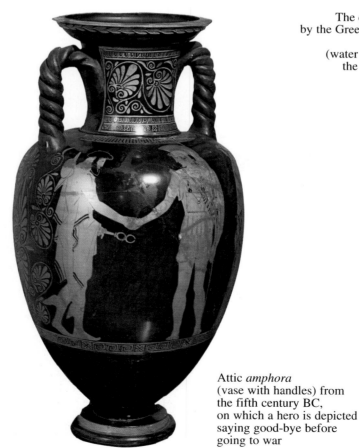

Attic *amphora* (vase with handles) from the fifth century BC, on which a hero is depicted saying good-bye before going to war

441

the difficult voyage home of one of the Greek princes, Odysseus of Ithaca, after the capture and destruction of Troy. It is more of a morality play, the good hero triumphing over his evil opponents. Just as in the *Iliad*, Odysseus's years of adventure are related in a very short time frame, in this case twenty-six days.

As the tale opens, we see the stress the prolonged absence of Odysseus has caused in his household. Greedy suitors are ruining his property as they court his wife Penelope. His son Telemachus sets out to discover what has become of his father, who has been gone for ten years without sending word. We then hear

from Odysseus himself during the last stages of his travels. On the island of Scheria, he tells King Alkinoös and Queen Areta about what has happened to him over the past ten years. This recital also serves to inform the reader of these adventures. Odysseus has had to face the man-eating giant Polyphemus, for instance, and the temptations of the goddess Calypso, who offered him immortality in return for his staying with her. The *Odyssey* ends with the almost simultaneous arrival of Odysseus and Telemachus on their home island of Ithaca. In his own palace, Odysseus learns what servants have remained loyal to him, then kills the suitors who have been besieging his supposed widow, Penelope. In the end, righteousness prevails and Odysseus is reunited with his beloved wife, his son, and his aged father.

While the *Iliad* describes in detail the wartime activities of the Achaeans, the *Odyssey* devotes attention to daily life in peacetime, depicting farmers, herders, servants, and noblemen. The epics paint a complete picture of society in those ancient times, including the constant emphasis on the contact between the mortal world and the world of the gods. The gods are ever-present in both the *Iliad* and the *Odyssey*, often as manipulative forces operating in the background. Both offer a wonderful portrayal of characters and emotions. We show here a single example of the great quality of these poems, namely the eternally beautiful description of Hector's farewell. Before Hector returns to battle he meets his wife Andromache. She has a premonition that her husband will not survive this time:

"So as he had come to the gates on his way through the great city, the Skaian gates, whereby he would issue into the plain, there at last his own generous wife came running to meet him, Andromache, the daughter of highhearted Eëtion; Eëtion, who had dwelt

Ruins of ancient Troy, in present-day Hisarlik (Turkey)

Part of a Greek relief, made in the third or second century BC. On the left, Homer is sitting on a throne, with *Oikoumène* (the world) and *Chronos* (time) behind him. Next to his throne are personifications of the *Iliad* and *Odyssey*. From the right, some allegorical figures are approaching the altar in the middle.

442

underneath wooded Plakos, in Thebe below Plakos, lord over the Kilikian people. It was his daughter who was given to Hector of the bronze helm. She came to him there, and beside her went an attendant carrying the boy in the fold of her bosom, a little child, only a baby, Hector's son, the admired, beautiful as a star shining, whom Hector called Skamandrios, but all of the others Astynax— lord of the city; since Hector alone saved Ilion.

"Hector smiled in silence as he looked on his son, but she, Andromache, stood close beside him, letting her tears fall, and clung to his hand and called him by name and spoke to him: 'Dearest, your own great strength will be your death, and you have no pity on your little son, nor on me, ill-starred, who soon must be your widow; for presently the Achaeans, gathering together, will set upon you and kill you; and for me it would be far better to sink into the earth when I have lost you, for there is no other consolation for me after you have gone to your destiny—only grief; since I have no father, no honored mother. It was brilliant Achilleus who slew my father, Eëtion, when he stormed the strong-founded citadel of the Kilikians, Thebe of the towering gates. He killed Eëtion but did not strip his armor, for his heart respected the dead man, but burned the body in all its elaborate war gear and piled a grave mound over it, and the nymphs of the mountains, daughters of Zeus of the aegis, planted elm trees about it. And they who were my seven brothers in the great house all went upon a single day down into the house of the death god, for swift-footed brilliant Achilleus slaughtered all of them as they were tending their white sheep and their lumbering oxen; and when he had led my mother, who was queen under wooded Plakos, here, along with all his other possessions, Achilleus released her again, accepting ransom beyond count, but Artemis of the showering arrows struck her down in the halls of her father. Hector, thus you are father to me, and my honored mother, you are my brother, and you it is who are my young husband. Please take pity upon me then, stay here on the rampart, that you may not leave your child an orphan, your wife a widow, but draw your people up by the fig tree, there where the city is openest to attack, and where the wall may be mounted. Three times their bravest came that way, and fought there to storm it about the two Aiantes and renowned Idomeneus, about the two Atreidai and the fighting son of Tydeus. Either some man well skilled in prophetic arts had spoken, or the very spirit within themselves had stirred them to the onslaught.'

"Then tall Hector of the shining helm answered her: 'All these things are in my mind also, lady; yet I would feel deep shame before the Trojans, and the Trojan women with trailing garments, if like a coward I were to shrink aside from the fighting; and the spirit will not let me, since I have learned to be valiant and to fight always among the foremost ranks of the Trojans, winning for my own self great glory, and for my father. For I know this thing well in my heart, and

Attic *oinochoe* (wine pitcher), dating from the end of the sixth century BC. The blind Cyclops Polyphemus is guarding the exit of his cave, in which he has imprisoned Odysseus and his comrades. As always, Odysseus thinks of a trick: on the left, he escapes by hiding under a sheep.

443

my mind knows it: there will come a day when sacred Ilion shall perish, and Priam, and the people of Priam of the strong ash spear. But it is not so much the pain to come of the Trojans that troubles me, not even of Priam the king nor Hekabe, not the thought of my brothers who in their numbers and valor shall drop in the dust under the hands of men who hate them, as troubles me the thought of you, when some bronze-armored Achaean leads you off, taking away your day of liberty, in tears; and in Argos you must work at the loom of another, and carry water from the spring Messeis or Hypereia, all unwilling, but strong will be the necessity

upon you; and some day seeing you shedding tears a man will say of you: "This is the wife of Hector, who was ever the bravest fighter of the Trojans, breakers of horses, in the days when they fought about Ilion." '

" 'So will one speak of you; and for you it will be yet a fresh grief, to be widowed of such a man who could fight off the day of your slavery. But may I be dead and the piled earth hide me under before I hear you crying and know by this that they drag you captive.'

"So speaking glorious Hector held out his arms to his baby, who shrank back to his fair-girdled nurse's bosom screaming, and frightened at the aspect of his own father, terrified as he saw the bronze and the crest with its horsehair, nodding dreadfully, as he thought, from the peak of the helmet. Then his beloved father laughed out, and his honored mother, and at once glorious Hector lifted from his head the helmet and laid it in all its shining upon the ground. Then taking up his dear son he tossed him about in his arms, and kissed him, and lifted his voice in prayer to Zeus and the other immortals: 'Zeus, and you other immortals, grant that this boy, who is my son, may be as I am, pre-eminent among the Trojans, great in strength, as am I, and rule strongly over Ilion; and some day let them say of him: "He is better by far than his father," as he comes in from the fighting; and let him kill his enemy and bring home the blooded spoils, and delight the heart of his mother.'

"So speaking he set his child again in the arms of his beloved wife, who took him back again to her fragrant bosom smiling in her tears; and her husband saw, and took pity upon her, and stroked her with his hand, and called her by name and spoke to her:

" 'Poor Andromache! Why does your heart sorrow so much for me? No man is going to hurl me to Hades, unless it is fated, but as for fate, I think that no man yet has escaped it once it has taken its first form, neither brave man nor coward. Go therefore back to our house, and take up your own work, the loom and the distaff, and see to it that your handmaidens ply their work also; but the men must see to the fighting, all men who are the people of Ilion, but I beyond others.'

"So glorious Hector spoke and again took up the helmet with its crest of horsehair, while his beloved wife went homeward, turning to look back on the way, letting the live tears fall."

Surrounded by servants, Penelope is mourning her disappeared husband Odysseus in her house. Terra-cotta plaque, dating from the first century AD

Odysseus's homecoming, painted on an Attic *skyphos* (beaker) from the fifth century BC. Odysseus has entered his own palace, disguised as a beggar. However, he is recognized by an old slave who washes Odysseus's feet as a sign of welcome and then identifies him by a scar on Odysseus's leg.

Crisis and Renaissance

The Dark Age and the Beginning of the Archaic Period

Mycenaean civilization, named for the ancient city Mycenae on the plain of Argolis, reached its peak on mainland Greece in the fourteenth century BC and declined in the late thirteenth and early twelfth centuries. Archaeologists subdivide the following centuries into the late Mycenaean or sub-Mycenaean period, lasting until the mid-eleventh century; the Dark Age, ca. 1050-750 BC; and the Archaic period, ca. 750-500 BC. Together, the eras were a formative time for a new Greek civilization that would leave its mark on a large part of the Mediterranean region and western Asia over the next century. Until 500 BC, however, it was not the Greeks who exercised influence; they themselves were influenced strongly by others, especially from the east.

One of these influences may have been the Hittite Empire, which dominated Asia Minor from about 1900 to 1200 BC. Hittite documents from the thirteenth and fourteenth centuries BC mention a region called Ahhiawa, identified by some scholars as Mycenae. Its seafaring people lived on the island of Lésvos (Lesbos) and on the edges of the Aegean Sea. There is evidence that Mycenaean Greeks visited Anatolia, Asia Minor, homeland of the Hittites, around 1400 BC.

The Dark Age gets its name from the dearth of information on the time and from the dim interlude it forms between the vigorous culture of the Bronze Age and the Archaic period.

Both the Greeks and the Mycenaeans Homer called Achaeans ranged the area Homer called Achaea. (In Greek mythology, Achaeans descended from Achaeus, the grandson of Hellen, ancestor of the Greeks, called Hellenes.)

Funeral scene, painted on an Attic vase from the sixth or fifth century BC

445

The *Iliad* and the *Odyssey* as Historical Sources

At issue is whether these epics, undoubtedly masterpieces of world literature, can be used as sources of information on the Dark Age of Greece as the Linear B tablets were for the Mycenaean world. These were found on clay tablets excavated on Crete and mainland Greece in the twentieth century AD and date from about 1400 to 1200 BC. The contents of the *Iliad* and the *Odyssey* were considered merely fantasy for a long time, but archaeological finds,

The so-called Aphrodite of Auxerre, probably made on Crete in the seventh century BC

especially those of Heinrich Schliemann (1822–1890), changed this opinion. Using the epics as a guide, he discovered the ruins of ancient Troy at the site of Hissarlik. No archaeological evidence points directly to events mentioned in the *Iliad* or the *Odyssey*. The written sources, as far as we can read them, are not conclusive; the Linear B scripts name no Homeric heroes.

Part of the credibility question stems from Schliemann himself, an amateur who left school at age fourteen. Fascinated by Homer's tales, he set out to prove them historically accurate, devoting the fortune he had made in business to that end. In 1870, he began digging in Turkey on the hill of Hissarlik. Excavating through several levels at the site, he claimed the second city from the bottom up to be Priam's Troy, although it was subsequently found to be of earlier origin. Priam's Troy was later discovered at a higher level. He turned his attention to Mycenae from 1876 to 1878, locating the tombs of the Mycenaean kings. He excavated at Ithaca later that year and at Orchomenus in 1881 and 1882. He uncovered the great palace at Tiryns in Greece between 1884 and 1885.

All this provided evidence of flourishing cultures in a distant past, but did not conclusively establish that the Trojan War ever took place. As knowledge of the Mycenaean world grew, especially after the decipherment of Linear B in 1952, it appeared that the society described in the epics did not really resemble the one excavated. The Mycenaean communities were large-scale and complex, while Homer describes small-scale, simple communities. Today it is generally assumed that the epics reflect the era of their writing and the centuries immediately preceding it, the Dark Age.

This does not mean that we can simply view the epics as a social history of the Dark Age. We have already said that the Homeric poems were for a long time handed down orally. This implies that elements from many different periods are mixed together in the text, from Mycenaean times to the eighth century BC. It is extremely difficult to distinguish which elements date from which period, and what may be merely fantasy—especially with regard to subjects for which there is no archaeological evidence. Although the *Iliad* and the *Odyssey* definitely tell us something more about life in the Dark Age, on which we have so little information, the oral character of the epic tradition means that we must always be very careful if we want to use the epics as a source of historical information.

The Dark Age

Archaeology reveals that Greece became impoverished and partially depopulated in the turbulent period following the collapse of Mycenaean culture. The number and the size of both settlements and burial grounds declined sharply in many places, indicating a reduction in population. The architecture and the earthenware show that the people lived in poverty. There was no technological advancement; only the use of iron increased during this period. Of greater significance is the complete disappearance of the complex society once centered on the palaces, with the concomitant loss of writing skills. The country appears to have broken down politically into small communities, each led by a *basileus*. This title is used

Ajax is carrying
the body of Achilles.
Detail of an Attic vase from the
sixth century BC

447

Dipylon vase in geometric style, made in the eighth century BC, painted with a mourning scene in which the deceased is surrounded by grieving people and hitched chariots

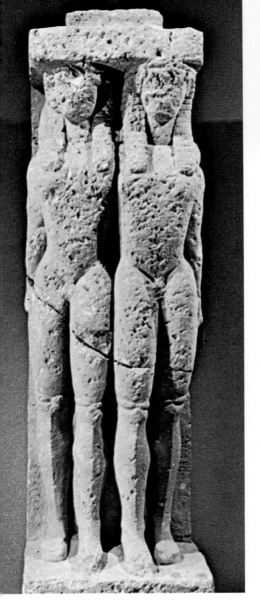

Limestone statue nearly 5 feet (1.5 meters) tall, made in the seventh century BC. The two figures have their arms around each other, a pose typical for Egyptian art of the time.

in Linear B texts to designate a village or district chief. In the palace hierarchy, the basileus was a subordinate figure, but in the Dark Age he was powerful, holding independent authority. In several communities, there was only a single basileus, giving the title the connotation of king. (Later, *basileus* was also the title used to designate the Byzantine emperor.)

The population evidently increased again in the ninth century BC, although factors that might foster the resurgence are unknown. (These could include a reduction in mortality rates and an increase in migration.) What is certain is that Greeks crossed over from the mainland about this time, via the islands in the Aegean Sea to the west coast of Asia Minor. (Earlier traces of migration at the end of the Bronze Age and the beginning of the Dark Age have also been found.) These ninth-century migrants included small groups of Greeks speaking the Doric dialect who moved from north to south and began to conquer parts of the Peloponnisos and Crete. Others from the mainland left for Cyprus, the Aegean Islands, and Asia Minor, possibly because the situation was better than on the Greek mainland. The isolated Attic peninsula functioned as a way station for people moving elsewhere.

Dialect was a significant factor in migration to Asia Minor, as people tended to settle into linguistic groups. Doric was the northwest dialect spoken all along the west of Greece and on the islands of Crete, Cos, and Rhodes as a result of Dorian conquest between 1200 and 1000 BC. It spread to Asia Minor as they settled there in the ninth century. The non-Doric dialects were Ionic, the language of Attica and the island of Évvoia; Aeolic, spoken in the northeast and in central Greece; and Arcado-Cyprian, the dialect spoken in Arcadia on the Peloponnisos and on Cyprus. Arcado-Cyprian is related to Mycenaean Greek, the dialect in which the Linear B inscriptions were written. The closeness of Arcado-Cyprian to the older Linear B may be due to the lack of migrant influence on the wild and rugged Arcadia. Cyprus, in contrast, served as a refuge for migrants from the mainland. The greatest contrast was between the Dorians and the Ionians, two groups who spoke different tongues, who had different customs and religious practices, and who each built up a position of power. This was a recipe for the conflict that was to come at a later date.

Over the course of the ninth century, representatives of three of these dialect groups settled in much of the coastal region of Asia Minor and on the islands off this coast. Those speaking the Aeolic dialect settled north of the Dardanelles on the northwest coast of Asia Minor down to Smyrna and on the island of Lésvos. Ionians settled on the central part of the coast from Smyrna to Miletus and on the islands of Chios and Samos. Dorians settled in the southern part between Halicarnassus and Rhodes and on the islands of Rhodes and Cos. Some of the many settlements created on these islands and in the coastal regions developed into important cities, in particular the twelve Ionian cities called the *dodeca polis* (twelve cities).

The migration to the islands and to Asia Minor stimulated further exploration, as well as the restoration of the customary trading routes. Linking large parts of the Mediterranean world with the Greek world, these routes had not been completely cut off in the Dark Age. Toward the end of the ninth century BC, Greek seafarers could once again be found in the harbors of northern Syria and Phoenicia. Cyprus, which had always remained predominantly Greek, played an important role in the reconstruction of this network. The restoration of

direct contacts with the east was extremely significant. The Greek world emerged from its temporary isolation and experienced such great change under eastern influences that a new era is defined as beginning about 750 BC. The new world that developed bore little resemblance to the Bronze Age civilization.

The Beginning of the Archaic Period

The Archaic period is named for a concept drawn from Greek art history; the word *archaic* comes from the Greek *archaikos*, meaning "ancient" or "old-fashioned," and is applied to the style that preceded classical Greek forms.

After about 800 BC, increased contact with the east brought the Greeks new ideas in the use of iron and bronze, pottery and sculpture, architecture, mythology, and religion. The reintroduction of writing, this time using an alphabet derived from Phoenician examples, was very important. It is not clear exactly when the Greeks started to adapt the Semitic alphabet to their own needs, but the oldest-known inscriptions using the new alphabet date from the

Cypriot *kernos* (ring-shaped vase) with four small amphoras and two animal heads, made around 1000 BC

449

Combat between two
heroes, one of whom is
probably Hercules, clothed
in the hide of a lion.
Detail of a Greek cup, made
in the sixth century BC

second half of the eighth century BC. After that, use of the alphabet spread rapidly and made possible the recording of the *Iliad* and *Odyssey*, in writing, although it is probable that the verses were originally composed orally.

The word *alphabet*, which comes from the first two letters of the Greek alphabet, *alpha* and *beta*, denotes a writing system in which a single character, or grapheme, represents a single sound, or phoneme. A syllabary, in contrast, uses a single symbol to represent one or more spoken sounds said as a unit or syllable. (Japanese uses two syllabaries.) Nonalphabetic systems of writing represent language by means of other types of graphemes, such as logograms, which are characters representing words, and characters with phonetic referents other than a single phoneme, such as characters representing syllables. Mesopotamian cuneiform used a combination of logographic and syllabic signs; Egyptian hieroglyphics used a combination of logographic signs, signs representing consonant groups, and signs representing single consonants. During the mid-second millennium BC, elements of the Egyptian hieroglyphic script were adapted to develop a script wherein each individual sound of a language (excluding vowel sounds) was represented by a single symbol—that is, an alphabet. This took place somewhere in the Syro-Palestinian region, and the inventors of this new script, the first alphabet, were speakers of a Semitic language. (Pictographic and ideographic systems are not considered alphabets or syllabaries until they are extended to represent sounds.)

The new alphabetic script differentiated rapidly into variant forms, as it was diffused among diverse peoples over the course of

the next several centuries; among the principal variants was the Northwest Semitic alphabet, from which nearly all alphabetic scripts in use today are ultimately descended. In the late Bronze Age, during the fourteenth and thirteenth centuries BC, a cuneiform alphabet of 30 letters was developed in the city of Ugarit on the coast of Syria. Cretan writing, which was in evidence nearby, used hieroglyphics. The new alphabet, like both of these, contained only consonants, no vowels. A short version of the Northwest Semitic alphabet, with 22 letters, was developed by the end of this period and was used to write the Phoenician language beginning in the eleventh century BC. From there it spread to neighboring regions in the Near East. This short Phoenician alphabet was borrowed by the Greeks by the eighth century BC. The Greeks modified it, adding two or more consonant symbols, depending on the dialect. They also began to use some symbols for consonants to represent vowel sounds. They began to write from left to right about 500 BC after a period of writing in either direction. As the Greek alphabet spread, it was adopted and modified by various Mediterranean peoples, including the Etruscans, the Umbrians, the Oscans, and the Romans. The last were the most influential, giving their adapted Roman alphabet, used to write in Latin, to all the tongues of western Europe.

The influence of the east on the Greek world is demonstrated by the extensive presence of Semitic words in the Greek vocabulary. They relate mainly to material objects like pots and pans or clothing, but no area of Greek life escaped this influence. It is so pervasive that the century between 750 and 650 BC has been called the "Orientalizing" (or eastern-influencing) period.

The Greek Polis

The *Iliad* and the *Odyssey* depict a Greek society that is primarily aristocratic in nature. There is mention of an unsophisticated tribal meeting, as well, but it had little influence. The epics also contain oblique references to the existence of realms that are similar to the city-states of a later peri-

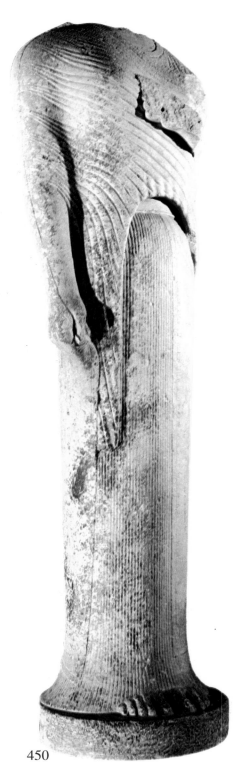

Korē (statue of a young woman), probably portraying Zeus's wife Hera. It dates from around 560 BC.

Mourning women are lamenting a dead man (possibly Achilles) on a stretcher. Detail of a Corinthian cup dating from about 570 BC

od of Greek history. These are apparently references to the author's own period, a time when the notion of the state was still developing. The state alluded to here was called a *polis* (plural *poleis*) by the Greeks. Common in the Greek world after the end of the Dark Age, the polis formed an autonomous administrative unit within a small territory, usually averaging between fifty and a hundred square miles (260 square kilometers), with a population between 2,500 and 4,500. Some poleis were relatively large and populous, particularly Sparta, Argos, Corinth, Athens, and Thebes. In Ionia, the large states were Samos, Miletus, and Ephesus. There were also independent states with a territory of fifteen square miles (39 square kilometers) and a population of only 250. Each polis had within its territory at least one place that was termed a city (confusingly enough also called a polis), no matter how small or unlike a city it actually was.

Each polis was autonomous. The freemen who were accounted its citizens organized their own political affairs. (The word *politics* is derived from *polis*.) For this purpose, they assembled in tribal meetings. However, real power in the Archaic period remained in the hands of the aristocracy, as it had before the creation of the polis. The *basileus*, who had ruled alone as king during the Dark Age, was now replaced in most cases by magistrates elected annually from the ranks of the nobles. These aristocrats owed their dominant position to a combination of prestige and wealth, expressed in the number of horses they owned and, after 700 BC, in their possession of bronze armor.

The armor carried by heavy infantry consisted of a helmet, a breastplate, shin plates, and a large round shield, the *hoplon*. The word for a heavily armed foot soldier, *hoplite*, was derived from the word for this shield. The hoplites fought in close ranks, in a battle array termed a *phalanx*. Armor was initially very expensive. The mobilization of a phalanx of heavily armed soldiers emphasized the dominance of the wealthy aristocracy over the poor masses. As bronze weapons were replaced with iron, aristocratic predominance in the army ended.

The emergence of the poleis took place at a time of rapid population growth. The rise in population fostered the conquest of sparsely populated regions, armed conflicts between neighboring poleis, and the further emigration of Greeks from the motherland. Sparta subjected the entire region of Laconia and began the conquest of neighboring Messenia in the eighth century; Argos extended its power over the Argolis region; and Athens united the peninsula of

Bronze lion
that once served as the
handle of a pitcher
(seventh century BC)

453

Attica into one polis. Emigration to places outside Greece led to what is termed Archaic Colonization (see pages 457-468).

Internal Relations within the Poleis

The colonization and the subsequent flourishing of trade, the growing contact, peaceful and otherwise, between the various poleis, the use of writing to record the laws and decrees of the polis community—all these developments had an influence on relations among the many small states of the Greek world. Social relations became more complex and the economic inequities increased. An elite of aristocrats and wealthy people (largely identical in the Archaic period) emerged, no longer obliged to work. They tried to reserve for themselves the riches obtained from their trade with the east. In several poleis, small groups of aristocrats managed to seize control and end the tribal meetings. The fundamental principle of the polis as a community of freemen was put to the test. The majority of citizens still had to work out of necessity and were often forced into some sort of dependent relationship with the richer landholders. These relationships frequently extorted poor citizens and even sold debtors into slavery. In Sparta and in some states on Crete, where Dorian immigrants had subdued the native population, aristocrats and ordinary citizens joined forces against the natives, forcing them to serve as laborers for the citizens, resulting in an even larger group behaving like an aristocracy.

In Sparta, attempts were made to solve internal tensions by making all citizens equal at the expense of a group who were excluded from citizenship and accorded no rights at all. In Athens and Corinth, tensions within the community led to internal political conflict. Brought on by rivalry between various aristocrats, such conflict was exacerbated by aristocrats seeking the support of nonelite members against fellow aristocrats. Individual aristocrats managed to seize power here and there and to install themselves as absolute sovereigns in a new kind of monarchy that the Greeks called *tyrannis* (tyranny).

Two mourning, armed warriors standing on their chariot attend a funeral. Detail of a Dipylon vase in geometric style, made around the middle of the eighth century BC

454

Statue of a
cavalryman, found on the
Acropolis of Athens
(ca. 500 BC)

and subsequently redistributed through the administration.

This complex system stands in striking contrast to the small kingdom of Odysseus as portrayed in the *Odyssey*. King Odysseus is a small-scale basileus with no bureaucracy to deal with. Relations are purely personal. The basileus takes care of his own household, which includes a number of dependent followers, and exchanges gifts with other leaders in order to strengthen mutual ties. The world of the epics exhibits no rigid hierarchy. In the real world, any minor king would have had to contend with the nobles in an informal council of advisors. The king therefore was not much more than a *primus inter pares* (first among equals). In the world of the Linear B tablets the basileus is subordinate to the wanax, but in the Homeric Age the basileus appears at the top of the social ladder.

Odysseus does have powerful nobles lurking in the vicinity. These men, or their sons, compete for the hand of his supposed widow (Odysseus is presumed dead, having been gone for ten years). They take over Odysseus's palace and plunder it. When the hero returns home, he punishes them severely for their insolence.

In this quotation from the *Iliad*, Odysseus speaks out against a certain Thersites, a common man, who dares to raise his voice to King Agamemnon:

"Thersites, you fool, hold your glib tongue! Stop arguing with kings! Not one of the Greeks at Troy is lower than you, so it befits you least of all to insult a king. If I witness your buffoonery once more then I will grab you and throw you out of the meeting with such a beating that you will flee weeping."

Odysseus underlines his words with a hard slap. This scene clearly illustrates the aristocratic standards of the society described in the *Iliad* and the *Odyssey*.

A *pyxis* (round, earthenware box) in geometric style, decorated with snakes and little horses on the lid. The design on the sides is a Greek cross and is the same design as the swastika. Found in a child's grave, dating from the middle of the eighth century BC

Power Relations in the Homeric World

The Linear B tablets describe a centralized administrative structure under the leadership of an official called a *wanax* (lord). This administration covered a relatively large area. Power was exercised by a hierarchy of people with authority through a bureaucratic structure in the palaces. There is evidence of a regional redistribution system. Products were collected in the palace

The so-called Temple of Ceres, probably dedicated to the goddess Athena and dating from around 500 BC. It was built in Doric style and can still be seen in Poseidonia (later called Paestum) in Campania on the Gulf of Salerno, Italy.

The Greek Expansion

Greek Colonization and Greek Poetry

From the second half of the eighth century to far into the sixth century BC, the Greeks founded dozens of settlements on the Mediterranean and Black Sea coasts. This is generally referred to as the Archaic Colonization. Expansion on this scale was not seen again until the time of Alexander the Great. The idea behind the new settlements was to create new, independent states. The colonies (the concept of colonization, though used here, is not strictly accurate) often inherited various social and political constructs, including religious cults, dialect, and their own versions of the alphabet, from their *metropoleis* (parent cities), but they were politically independent.

A newly founded *polis* (singular of *poleis*) was called an *apoikia* by the Greeks; it means "settlement elsewhere." *Emporia* (trading posts) dependent on the original poleis were frequently founded at the same time. Al Mina on the Syrian coast and Naucratis in the Egyptian Nile Delta are two of the most famous Greek emporia. The distinction between the two is not always clear-cut. An apoikia may have started out as an emporion and then experienced a transition to colonial status. Ready-made poleis with everything organized and arranged would certainly not have been founded in the early phase of the Archaic Colonization. The home poleis in Greece and in Asia Minor were only just beginning to develop themselves. A trading outpost would often have

457

been established first, with colonists following at a later stage. The average apoikia was probably set up with no more than one or two hundred people. Several poleis in the motherland sent out four or five groups of emigrants within a single generation. Given the size of the population involved, these groups could never have been very large.

The metropolis was held in esteem by its colonies, and the religious customs of the parent city preserved in spite of any political differences. The metropolis and the daughter poleis sent official envoys to each other's religious festivals. Their special relationship was sometimes demonstrated by the provision of military aid to the colony. For instance, Corinth helped the city of Syracuse to fight the Athenians in Sicily, because Syracuse was its colony. In this way, several other wars between the original Greek cities were resolved.

Destinations

Colonies fanned out in all directions from metropoleis on the Greek mainland, as well as from the new colonies themselves at a later stage. The new settlements were situated on the Aegean Islands along the northern coast of the Aegean Sea; on the northern coast of Asia Minor along the Hellespont and Bosporus; around the Black Sea, especially on the Crimea, and at the foot of the Caucasus Mountains; on the North African coast in Cyrene (in what is now Libya); on Sicily and in southern Italy; on the south coast of France; and on the northeastern coast of Spain. Some of the most well-known colonies include Syracuse, Catania, Akragas, and Himera on Sicily; Tarentum, Metapontion, Sybaris, Croton, Neapolis (Naples), and Cymae in southern Italy; Massilia (Marseille) in southern France; and Byzantion (Byzantium, later Constantinople and Istanbul) on the Bosporus. The Greek presence was so dominant, particularly in Sicily and southern Italy, that this area was sometimes known as *Magna Grecia*, or Greater Greece.

It is significant to look at the areas where no new colonies were founded. There were none on the east coast of the Mediterranean because that region was already well occupied. There were none on a large section of the North African coast because of the dominance of Egypt. The territory to the west of

Greek warriors during a fight, painted on a *kylix* (cup)

Charioteer with a four-in-hand, depicted on an amphora that was handed out as a prize at the Panathenaic Games (fifth century BC)

Greek bowl with
a picture of Pallas Athena
standing between
two warriors

Cyrene was entirely in the hands of the Phoenicians. The same applied to the western part of Sicily, the whole of Sardinia, the smaller islands in the western Mediterranean, and a large part of the Spanish coast.

In the first two or three centuries after 1000 BC—before the time of the Greeks—it was the Phoenicians, coming from what is now Lebanon, who explored the coasts of the Mediterranean as far as Spain. They founded trading posts and colonies in various places. Their colony Carthage (*Carthadasht* means "New City" in Phoenician) on the north coast of Africa developed into a major commercial and political power. It competed fiercely with the Greeks in the western part of the Mediterranean, the cause of frequent clashes. *Neapolis* (also "New City") became a major port on the Italian Peninsula.

When a group of emigrants boarded a ship, or, as some sources imply, were forced to board, they were already well prepared. They knew where they wanted to go, they had consulted an oracle before setting out to ensure a favorable outcome to the voyage, and they had chosen a leader. At least, that is what they were supposed to do. Colonies that did not possess the text of an oracle, or that could not point out the tomb of their original founder, often produced the necessary forgeries in order to ensure their standing.

The first order of business for the immigrants was to drive the native population away, if there was one. It is not certain whether it was common practice to subdue the original inhabitants and bind them in

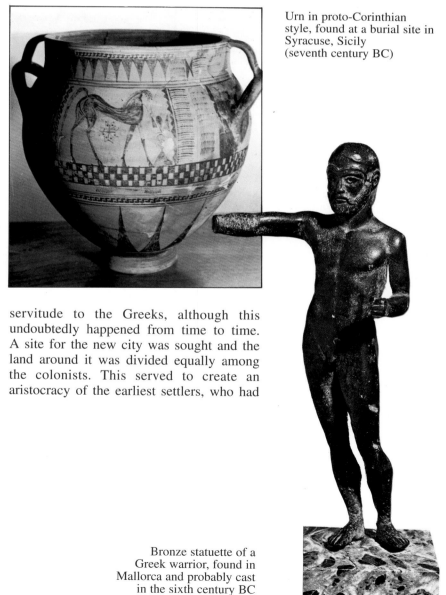

Urn in proto-Corinthian
style, found at a burial site in
Syracuse, Sicily
(seventh century BC)

servitude to the Greeks, although this undoubtedly happened from time to time. A site for the new city was sought and the land around it was divided equally among the colonists. This served to create an aristocracy of the earliest settlers, who had

Bronze statuette of a
Greek warrior, found in
Mallorca and probably cast
in the sixth century BC

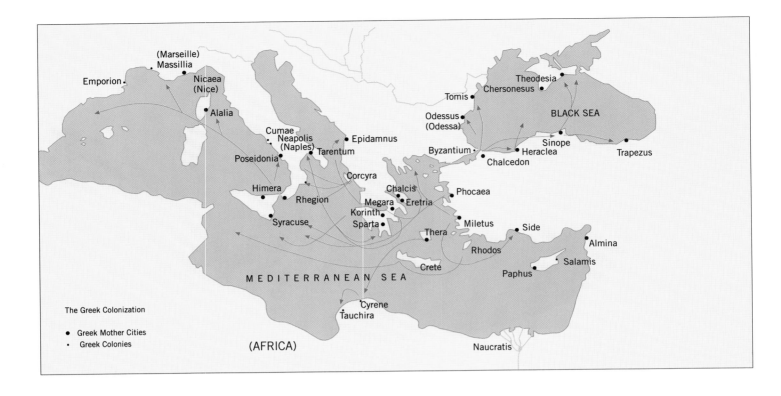

Map of the Greek colonization of the Mediterranean

The coast near the harbor of Emporion (sixth century BC), a Greek colony situated in the northeast of Spain. The ancient harbor has become completely silted up, but the Hellenistic jetty is still there.

first choice and first rights. Immigrants arriving later would probably have been granted civil rights and a small piece of land, but would certainly have been accorded subordinate positions in society. This explains the fairly extensive elite groups that occupied the aristocratic councils in many colonies. It is not clear where the women in the colonies came from; they may have been sent for from the parent city or they may have been sought (or abducted) from neighboring regions.

Causes and Consequences

If a colony developed into a more permanent community, it usually took the form of an agricultural settlement based on the pattern of the motherland. Arable land was of primary importance, regardless of how much trading took place in a colony. Many Greek colonies were founded in regions with good agricultural land. The Archaic colonization is therefore attributed to the shortage of land in the homeland.

In a passage in the *Odyssey*, Odysseus tells about an island near the land of an uncivilized giant people, the Cyclopes. He says, "The Cyclopes have no ruddy vessels, no shipbuilders to build them ships with many benches, ships with which so much can be accomplished by sailing to distant cities, as so often people cross the sea to visit one another. Such people would also have been able to cultivate this island properly."

This last sentence reveals something about the Greek sea voyager in the Archaic period, always looking out for promising land that might be suitable for future settlement. Many of the emigrants were probably forced to travel for economic reasons. This factor would seem to have applied less to their aristocratic and wealthier leaders. They might have left the parent city for political reasons or with the intent of starting anew elsewhere.

The natural consequence of Greek colonization was not only a migration of people but a migration of their entire culture, their technological skills, their customs, their religion, and their concepts and attitudes. The Greeks brought everything with them, from specific agricultural methods and crops like the olive and the grape to an entire hierarchy of gods. The export of culture from the Aegean region to the Italian region was of great significance to the further progress of European history. The colonies of Magna Grecia formed a bridge between east and west, as the Mycenaeans and the Phoenicians had done before them.

An excellent example of this is Pithecussae on Ischia, an island in the bay of Naples. Pithecussae, where excavations have been carried out since the 1950s AD, was founded by people from the Aegean island of Évvoia. Certainly not a typical colony, it was a very early settlement located right on the northern frontier of what was later the Greek world. It was also not completely Greek. It appears to have started as an emporion and developed into an apoikia at a later date. Pithecussae seems to have had not only a Greek, but also a Semitic presence. It demonstrates how the Greek settlements functioned as a corridor through which eastern influences reached the Iron Age cultures of Italy, stimulating major changes. In the seventh and sixth centuries BC, under the influence of the Greeks, a Mediterranean urban culture began to take root in the Etruscan region of central Italy.

Colonization not only generated changes in the regions occupied by the Greeks, the colonies themselves stimulated developments in the motherland. The foundation of strong and independent colonies overseas boosted trade considerably. Grain from Sicily and southern Russia was exported to Greece. Wine, bronze plate, and high-quality pottery went from the motherland to the colonies. The Greeks there often resold these products to indigenous rulers living inland, Scythian, Etruscan, and Celtic, being a few. Pottery finds have been particularly helpful to contemporary archaeologists, enabling them to map out trade movements and contacts between Greeks and non-Greeks. It has been learned that Phoenician-Carthaginian and Greek traders supplied bronze artifacts, pottery, wine, and other luxury articles via intermediaries to chieftains living in remote inland parts of western and central Europe, exchanging these articles for silver, tin, or slaves. A beautiful Greek

bronze *krater* (for mixing wine with water) came from the tomb of a ruler in Vix in the Seine valley.

Poetry Dating from the Colonial Era
Around 650 BC, the poet Archilochus left his birthplace on the island of Paros for Thasos, an island off the Thracian coast, where inhabitants of Paros had founded a colony earlier that century, and where the Greeks were continuously fighting with the Thracians in mid-century.

Corinthian *aryballos*
(oil flask),
shaped as a helmeted soldier

461

The ruins of Neapolis,
the ancient Greek port of
Emporion, situated
on the mainland south of the
harbor

Archilochus lamented his stay in the "triply dreadful city of Thasos," where, as he put it, "the dregs of the entire Greek nation" came together to fight "the Thracian dogs. Thasos rises up like the back of a donkey, covered with rugged pine forests; it is not beautiful, charming and seductive like the land around the Siris." The Siris was a river in southern Italy, between Sybaris and Metapontion, where a colony was founded in approximately 675 BC by the Ionians from Colophon.

This view of Thasos not only provides a fascinating glimpse into the mind of the Greek colonist, with his idealistic view of the paradise over the horizon and with his disappointments, it also offers a very personal impression. Archilochus represents, in a period of great change in the Greek world, both the old aristocratic society and the world of the "pirates," who were certainly present in the colonies, if only in the early stage of their existence. He belongs to both worlds, or to neither, and that gives him the freedom to think and to speak his mind through his poems. Thus, in this period of geographical expansion by the Greeks, there is also evidence of their intellectual exploration.

The Homeric epics acquired their definitive form around 700 BC. Their verses were widely recited and eventually displaced other forms of poetry, though the work of the poet Hesiod from Boeotia retained the traditional epic form. Not an aristocrat, but a well-to-do farmer, he lived around 700 BC. This makes his work exceptional for that time and particularly interesting. Even though the form was traditional, some of the content of his poetry was novel in the Greek world. For instance, the poet sometimes featured himself in his work. Hesiod wrote a long didactic poem on farming, called *Works and Days*, and a similarly didactic poem on the origin of the gods and their relations to each other, the *Theogony*.

However, the really new literature came from the poets of the seventh and sixth centuries, who were no longer bound by the traditional form of epic verse but could choose their own poetic structure. They wrote poems that were recited at drinking sessions or at feasts, sometimes commissioned by aristocrats, occasionally by tyrants. On other occasions, they wrote for the entire polis community, producing, for example, choral songs to be performed at religious festivals.

According to ancient reviews, the greatest

Fragment of a silver chariot decoration, made in Ionia in the sixth century BC. The riders are probably Amazons, legendary female warriors who were renowned for their fighting spirit.

writer of choral songs was the poet Alcman, who dated from around the second half of the seventh century. Alcman was probably a Greek from Asia Minor who worked as a poet in Sparta, where he wrote songs for the choirs, girl choirs in particular, that performed during feasts and ceremonies. In addition to many fragments, we have a substantial section of one of Alcman's *partheneia*, or "virgin songs," thanks to the chance find of a papyrus from the first century AD. This provides a unique example of what was heard during religious occasions in Sparta, when the girls first sang about mythological tales and then about themselves. Without this papyrus, we would have known nothing about this type of poetry.

Another style is called the *elegy*. This is a poem with a specific verse form intended for a solo singer rather than a choir. Tyrtaeus was a Spartan elegiac poet of the seventh century; fragments of his marching songs and battle songs from the time of the conquest of Messenia still remain. Another important writer of elegies was Solon, the Athenian lawgiver (see pages 478-480). A younger contemporary of Solon was Theognis of Megara. Unfortunately, many poems by other writers, including Tyrtaeus and Solon and other much later poets, have been ascribed to Theognis, making it difficult to establish what is original and what is not.

However, the poems now attributed to the

Small alabaster jars, made in the eastern Mediterranean and found in Emporion

Ruins of a Doric temple on Sicily

real Theognis throw an interesting light on the period in which he lived, the second half of the sixth century. Theognis was a conservative, somewhat reactionary nobleman, who viewed the social changes of that time with great sorrow:

"Dear Cyrnus, our city is still a city, but the population is different; those who used to know nothing of law and order, but who used to live like deer outside the city walls wearing shabby goatskins, those people are now the notables and the former notables are now the inferiors. Whoever can bear such a spectacle?"

Archilochus was the grand master of the

View of the peninsula of Attica. The peninsula served as a bulwark for the Ionians.

465

poetic style called iambic verse, named after the iambic rhythm in which it is written. It uses a pattern of a short (or unstressed) syllable followed by a long (or stressed) syllable. This meter closely approximates spoken language. This informality is reflected in the content of the poems. They are about everyday life and personal feelings and are often mocking or sarcastic. Through them, Archilochus manages to convey his unique and individual character. Another poet from

Ruins of the Greek colony of Elea, founded in the sixth century BC in Campania, south of Naples. The Romans later called the city Velia.

the seventh century, Semonides, is a special case. Though little is known about him, one remarkable poem he wrote, an excerpt of which is given here, illustrates attitudes with respect to women during the Archaic period:

"In the beginning the god created the characters of different types of women. One type of woman is made like a bristly boar. An untidy mess fills her house. . . . She sits unwashed in filthy clothes amid the garbage and stuffs herself with food. Another type is modeled on the cunning fox, able to turn her hand to anything. She misses nothing which may be to her advantage or disadvantage. She can even argue that straight is bent and bent is straight. . . . The third type is like a swift dog, who wants to hear and to know

everything and who lurks everywhere. . . . No man can stop her, not by means of threats and not even if he knocks out her teeth with a stone in a fit of rage, and not by using friendly words. The fourth type is molded out of clay by the gods and handed straight to the man. She is like a clay doll. She does not know the first thing about anything and can do nothing with her hands except eat. Even if the god produces a bitter winter, she is too slow-witted to pull her chair closer to the fire. The fifth woman resembles the sea and has two natures in one mind. One moment she laughs and is happy and every stranger who enters her home praises her . . . and the next moment she is unbearable . . . unapproachable, raging like a bitch protecting her young. She is unfriendly and snarls at both friend and foe. . . . The sixth type is like a horse with a soft mane. She tries to avoid drudgery and effort, she touches no grindstone, she lifts no sieve, she removes no dirt from the house. She avoids the oven and the hearth for fear of soot . . . she washes herself two or three times a day and applies myrrh to her skin. Her hair is always well brushed and adorned with roses. Such a woman is wonderful to look at—for others, at least—but disastrous to keep, unless she is owned by a tyrant or a king who likes to flaunt such beauty. The seventh type is an ape. This is undoubtedly the worst calamity given to man by Zeus. She is repulsive to look at; the entire city mocks her . . . wretched is the man who must embrace her, for she is also full of tricks, as an ape tends to be, and these tricks are definitely not amusing. She never tries to oblige but always aims to cause as much damage as possible for others. But the eighth type of woman is like a bee. It is a lucky man who owns her. She alone is untainted. Life is favorable under her care. She lovingly accompanies her affectionate husband on the journey of life and bears handsome, noble children. . . . It does not please her to sit with other women and join in their torrid conversations. Such a woman is the most glorious and wonderful gift from Zeus. But all other types are, as planned by Zeus, an indestructible disaster for men."

Sappho and Alcaeus

The next group consists of the so-called Lesbian lyrists, writers of lyric poetry from the island of Lésvos. The poet Alcaeus from Mytilene, born around 620 BC, wrote verses with a personal flavor about contemporary politics, in which he played an active role. He also wrote hymns to the gods, love songs, and drinking songs. The poetess Sappho was a contemporary of Alcaeus and also from the same place. Sappho wrote very personal,

The so-called
Demeter of Knidos,
a statue of the
goddess Demeter dating
from around 350 BC

Portrait of the poetess
Sappho, who lived on the
island of Lésvos with
her pupils around
600 BC

often passionate lyric verses. Unfortunately only two nearly intact poems by Sappho and fragments of the rest of her work have been preserved. Tradition has it that she taught "the noblest girls from Lésvos and Ionia." We can assume that she taught subjects like poetry, music, and dance, these skills being needed by the girls with a view to religious ceremonies. In some poems, the girls are spoken to in words that belong in the sphere of Greek homosexuality. In order to understand this, we must first view it in a broader context.

Male homosexuality in the Greek world involved the relationship of a young, typically still unmarried man in his twenties with a boy in his teens. The older partner functioned as a protector, a mentor, and a teacher for the younger boy. Besides the physical-sexual element, the partnership incorporated educational aspects, guidance into adulthood, and personality development. The relationship ended in principle when the older of the two married or when the younger became an adult. As far as we know, in Athens this pattern was mainly limited to the (semi-) aristocratic circle, belonging to the initiation phase of the Athenian upper classes. However, in Dorian communities like Sparta this was a general, institutionalized phenomenon, part of the initiation of every warrior.

Sappho's relationships with young girls should be considered in the same light. This was an initiation process with a sexual element. Though in the poetry of Alcman girls praise their female chorus leaders in what appears to be love poetry, this is not necessarily taken to indicate homosexuality. Sappho addressed her poems to girls who were about to get married; it was not until the first century AD that her poetry was viewed in a purely erotic light.

Corinthian *aryballos*
(oil flask) with a picture of
a horseman,
made in the late seventh
century BC

468

The inside of a Laconian bowl (sixth century BC). Two Spartan warriors carry a wounded mate home; at the bottom are two fighting cocks.

Sparta and Athens

A Comparison of Two Greek City-states

Sparta was a *polis* (city-state) situated in the southern part of the Peloponnisos. The southern part of that peninsula is geographically divided into two areas, Laconia, which is the valley of the Eurotas River, and Messenia, the basin of the Pamisos River. These two fertile regions are separated from each other by the high Taygetus Mountains, which run from north to south.

In the tenth century BC, the Eurotas Plain was captured by a small group of Greek warriors who spoke the Doric dialect. Subduing the native population, the invaders moved into several villages grouped near the hills in the center of the plain, forming the settlement of Sparta. Only a few details are known about its development over the next few centuries, but the Spartan regime apparently differed considerably from that in other Greek *poleis* (city-states). The conquering people, now called Spartans, were the warriors, led by two kings; the conquered consisted of *helots*, or serfs, and *perioikoi*, neighboring freemen who recognized the authority of the Spartan kings. Sparta continued to expand its territory. By the eighth century BC, there was insufficient land in Laconia to provide a reasonable living for all the warriors of the

growing population. The highly fertile plain of neighboring Messenia offered a solution. After a lengthy war, the Spartans took it over completely at the end of the seventh century. Their original settlement in the Eurotas Valley remained the heart of the state, while Messenia was regarded as occupied territory.

The poet Tyrtaeus wrote battle songs for Sparta during this period. His verses constitute the oldest written record of its history. He described the rewards that would be had when all Messenians were made into helots: "Like heavily laden donkeys, they will be forced by hard means to hand over to their masters half of what they harvest in their fields." That is precisely what happened.

Helots

Helots were indigenous people of the Eurotas Plain who were enslaved by the Dorian conquerors of Sparta (and later, Messenia). They comprised the lowest of four social classes in the state. The others were the *perioikoi* (neighbors), the warriors, and the kings. Kings were also warriors.

The helots functioned as slaves, performing all agricultural work while their Spartan masters concentrated on military matters. In time of war, they could be used to row the long galleys or as low-ranking soldiers in the field. The helots were accorded no civil rights but, in contrast to slaves, they were not the property of individual Spartans. Owned by the state, they could not be bought and sold individually. Best described as state slaves, they belonged with particular plots of land. Such land was allocated, complete with helots, to a Spartan for his sustenance. He was not permitted to sell "his" helots or to release them. He was probably not allowed to kill them. The state, rather than the individual Spartans, determined the percentage of the harvest the helots had to hand over to their masters. They were allowed to keep for themselves what they harvested over that amount.

There were some legal ways for helots to secure their freedom. A Spartan father could adopt his children by a helot mother, making Spartan citizens of the children. In addition, from the fifth century on, helots could earn the status of freemen by fighting with the Spartans as full-fledged soldiers in wartime. In neither case could the helot acquire full Spartan civil rights.

The helots were by no means always well treated. The Spartans were a minority in their own state and, always fearful of an uprising, kept the helots firmly under control through systematic humiliation and intimidation. One manifestation of that was the custom of *krypteia*, the killing of helots by young Spartans hiding in the wilderness. This seems to have been a typical boy's initiation ritual, isolation followed by the killing of an "enemy." The custom was probably not widely practiced, as killing your own laborers on a large scale is not very sensible. Only a few murders would have been required to intimidate them. The repression of helots, probably greater in Messenia than in

Landscape in the west of Messenia, with the isle of Proti in the background

‹ Bust of Lycurgus, the famous Spartan legislator who lived in the seventh century BC

471

Ionian coin,
with the inscription for the
town of Clazomenae

Laconia, no doubt increased after a major helot rebellion in the first half of the fifth century BC. An estimated two thousand helots, freed in order to serve as soldiers for Sparta in the Peloponnesian War (431-404 BC), were killed by secret assassins to forestall plotting against their rulers.

Perioikoi

The other group that was not entitled to Spartan civil rights were the *perioikoi* (neighbors). Probably pre-Dorian inhabitants of the area, like the helots, these people lived on the outskirts of the polis, particularly to the south, as freemen. Although they had no political rights, their communities were internally autonomous. They had to answer to Sparta only in matters of external interest. Sparta had little interest in them in times of peace, but in times of war they were expected to supply soldiers. Most perioikoi were farmers. The few who were craftsmen and traders were of particular interest to the Spartans who practiced neither themselves. In similar fashion to the way they let the helots work the land, the Spartans left matters of craft and trade to the perioikoi.

The Lycurgan Constitution

The constitution of Sparta has traditionally been attributed to the lawgiver Lycurgus, although his actual existence was doubted even in ancient times. The constitution is not the work of one man, but rather the result of an evolutionary process and an adaptation to circumstances. After the conquest of Messenia, a number of changes probably took place in Spartan society. Quite likely, the basic administrative and social structure in place since the conquest of Laconia would have continued, but would have been adapted and systematized in the late seventh and early sixth centuries. The resulting state can be termed Lycurgan Sparta for purposes of distinction from the earlier society, without assuming that one individual named Lycurgus was responsible for all the changes.

Sparta's political institutions were not all attributable to Lycurgus. Pre-Lycurgan traditions include the simultaneous rule of two kings. Except for their joint command of the army, most of their functions were purely honorary. They received large shares of any war booty, enjoyed numerous privileges, and carried out various religious tasks. Real power, however, lay not with the kings, but with the public assembly, the council, and the magistrates.

Apella

The public assembly, called *apella*, was a

472   Burial scene, detail of a Attic vase

meeting of all adult warriors with Spartan civil rights. These, of course, did not include the helots and the perioikoi. It is not clear how much power this meeting really had as a democratic voice for all citizens. The apella could not take initiative, since the meetings were prepared by the *gerousia* (council of elders), twenty-eight men aged sixty and above, all from the best families. The apella was also unable to make amendments. Voting took place by means of booing or cheering, the deciding factor being the group that made the most noise.

The volume of sound was judged by the five *ephors*, the highest magistrates in the polis, where the real authority lay. The five ephors were the most important magistrates, elected by and from the tribal meeting. These five men, supervising the entire state of affairs in Sparta, constituted the actual government. They held meetings with the gerousia, influencing their choice of the agenda items to be discussed at the general meeting, or apella. The pair of kings and the ephors might have many points of disagreement, but the ephors had the last word. They could charge the kings with misconduct, fine them, dethrone them, and sentence them to exile. The kings and the ephors swore an oath every month; the kings pledged to observe the laws and the ephors promised in return to defend the kingdom.

Spartan Militarism and Conservatism

From the sixth century BC on, Spartan society became increasingly rigid. In Lycurgan Sparta everything was focused on the maintenance of a powerful army and the ideal of the equality of all citizens. Everything considered new and strange was rejected. Sparta became an introverted community where change was seen as undesirable and strangers were not welcomed. The Spartan self-image, and the image perceived by outsiders, became increasingly austere, strict, and conservative. The preservation of the supposed ordinance of Lycurgus turned into an ideology that Sparta used to distinguish itself from other Greek poleis.

The word *spartan* today refers to the external features of this Spartan ideology. Initially rooted in the primacy accorded the military and the state over the needs of the individual, it carries a connotation of strict austerity in all aspects of lifestyle.

A symbol of this austerity is the notorious "black soup" made from pig's blood, pork, salt, and vinegar. The writer Plutarch says in his biography of Lycurgus:

"One of the means of eradicating excess and refinement was the food in the barracks. There, the plain meals eaten by the Spartans

were prescribed by law. Fifteen men sat at each table, and each of these men had to supply his monthly contribution; a measure of grain, five pounds of cheese, two and a half pounds of figs, plus money to buy meat and fish. The most famous Spartan dish was the black soup. The older men usually sat together on one side of the table to eat their

Picture of a woman fastening her sandals, painted on an Attic amphora (end of the sixth century BC)

473

Portrait of Solon, one of the most important politicians in sixth-century Athens

of the program, although they participated in athletics until they reached the age of eighteen—undressed, and together with the boys, to the amazement of other Greeks. At the age of twelve, the boys were separated permanently from their mothers to begin their rugged life in the barracks. Everything was focused on hardening the future soldiers. Men and women did not live together but stayed in separate male or female quarters. Marriage was secondary to state interests, but couples were permitted to share a room at night. Healthy future warriors and mothers of warriors needed to be born. For this reason, the marriage age for girls was higher than elsewhere in the Greek world and great attention was devoted to the physical education of girls. Children with any defects whatsoever were left to die in the mountains. Women were "loaned" to powerful fellow Spartans in the hope of producing even stronger children.

In many respects, Spartan life was quite austere. The settlement of Sparta was no more than a collection of neighboring villages, not worthy of being called a city. With the exception of a few temples and *stoas* (sheltered promenades), there were no stone buildings, only huts. There were no coins and no memorial stones. The art of poetry, which had flourished in the seventh and sixth centuries, died away. The once-famous bronze and pottery work of Laconia was replaced by the production of a few shabby utensils.

black soup, leaving the meat for the younger men."

The Spartan upbringing attracted the interest of other Greeks right from the early days. Children aged seven took part in the collective education compulsory for all Spartan boys. The girls probably only followed part

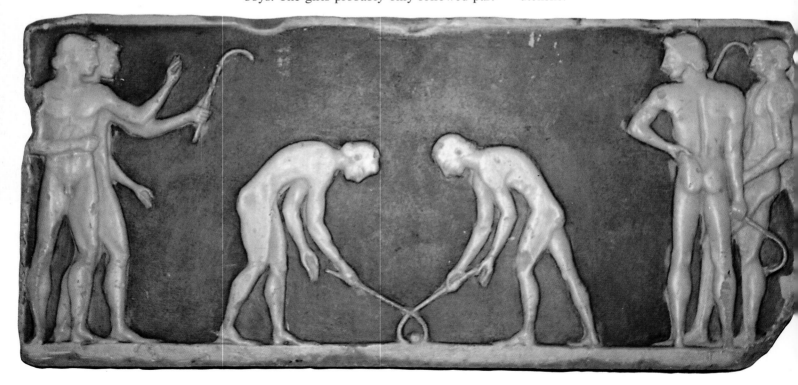

474   Marble relief (dating from around 500 BC) depicting a group of boys playing a game similar to hockey

The island of Delos

Music and dance remained very important in the religious life of Sparta, but creativity was evidently lacking in those fields, as well. Only in the military field did Sparta play a prominent role in Greece. During the Persian War, it assumed the military leadership almost automatically. The heroic death of King Leonidas and his followers in the pass of Thermopylae reinforced Sparta's claim to this leadership. However, there were some in the ancient world (and in later times) who admired Sparta not only for its military strength, but also for its fine example of virtue, honesty, austerity, and fidelity. The Greek philosopher Plato declared that Sparta came closest to his concept of the ideal state. Athens surely has a far better claim.

Athens and Its Early History

The polis Athens consisted of the city of Athens and the region surrounding it, the Attic Peninsula on the east coast of Greece. Attica is mountainous and dry but has a number of reasonably fertile plains and good

Marble relief (made around 510 BC) on which two young men are wrestling. Another athlete is standing to their left; the man on the right is a spear thrower.

natural harbors. The region is separated from central Greece and from the Corinthian isthmus by virtually impassable mountains. Attica's inhabitants have always had strong links with the sea that encloses it on two sides. People and goods came to the region by sea. The sea provided their own access to distant worlds.

Athens originated as a Mycenaean settlement on and around the Acropolis, a rock outcropping that lies in the middle of the largest plain of Attica. It is not known if the whole of Attica formed a political unit in that early period. According to legend, Theseus united twelve Attican villages into one polis. Whether or not this has any basis in historical fact cannot be proven. It can, however, be established that the Mycenaean fortress on the Acropolis was never destroyed and that Athens was continuously inhabited from the late Helladic period, through the Dark Age, to the Archaic period. There is, therefore, a grain of truth in the later claim by the Athenians that they were the real indigenous Greeks whose domain had never been conquered by strangers. Certainly in terms of

military strategy, the position of Athens was extremely favorable. Attica is a remote region hidden behind high mountains. The Acropolis provided a safe refuge in the plain of Athens. The sea was a mere four miles (6.5 kilometers) away.

Aristocratic Athens

In terms of the social and political structure of the polis, Athens followed the pattern of many of the other Greek city-states. Three social groups could be distinguished. Dominating the others were the *hippeis* (horsemen or knights). These were aristocrats, the group owning the most land, which was usually worked by their tenants. In the second rank were the *zeugitai*, owners of a *zeugos* (a yoke or pair of oxen). These were farmers who owned enough land to be economically independent. Below them both were the *thetes*, small farmers and day laborers. In principle, all these groups, from the aristocrats to the landless, were Athenian citizens. This was fairly unusual, as landownership and civil rights were linked in many neighboring areas. Beginning in the seventh

century BC or earlier, Athens had a board of nine magistrates elected annually, called the *archons*. These archons were always aristocrats. Ex-archons became members of the *areopagus*, a council named after the place where it convened, the *Areos Pagos* or hill of the god Ares.

Athens also experienced enormous social tension. Poor small farmers lost their land to richer landholders and were subsequently forced to rent farmland in exchange for a sixth of the yield, a high price in the relatively infertile and dry Attica. Anyone who could not pay his rent was declared a debtor, a situation that could easily lead to debt slavery. Creditors were merciless in enforcing their claims against debtors. People who could not pay were often sold into slavery, together with their wives and children. There are even records of poor Athenian citizens being sold into slavery abroad by their creditors. This conflicts greatly with the notion that all Athenians had equal rights and privileges in the polis. Growing discontent

The Terrace of the Lions in front of the temple of Apollo on the island of Delos. Sixteen marble lions once stood here, donated as votive gifts to Apollo by the citizens of Naxos at the end of the seventh century BC.

brought with it a danger of unrest. The perpetual competition among the aristocrats led to fear that one of them might take advantage of the situation to seize power. This was the motivation for their work toward a solution.

Solon

One way of tackling the problems was to reform the law. This also happened in several other poleis; evidently social unrest was seen as a collapse of the system of law. This measure was also taken in Athens, with the appointment of Solon as an archon with special powers at the beginning of the sixth century BC. There can be no doubt as to the existence of the lawgiver Solon, in contrast to Lycurgus, as the sources are too specific. Solon is the first person in Athenian history of whom we can form a clear picture, partly thanks to several verses written by Solon himself. At a later date he was idealized as the outstanding example of a wise lawgiver, and all kinds of institutions and laws from a later period were also attributed to him. However, it was definitely Solon who put an end to the worst abuses in Athens.

One of Solon's first decisions was to invite

An Attic
black-figured *kylix*
(drinking cup),
dating from about
550 BC

a large number of emigrants and exiles to return to Athens. Some of these had been banished from the country for political reasons. Others had fled due to the huge burden of debt strangling the tenant farmers. The primary condition for the return of this last group was the cancellation of all their debts. Solon succeeded in obtaining this, getting all debts canceled for which the person or the land of the debtor was pledged as security. He abolished debt slavery, making it no longer possible for someone to guarantee a debt with his own person. Freedom was purchased for the debt slaves who could be traced.

Solon speaks of his reforms in these verses: "I gave Athens, divine city, back its sons; men who were sold either lawfully or unlawfully; men who were driven from their native country by poverty; vagrants who had almost forgotten how to speak their own language. I did all this by using the laws and the powers given to me."

Whether something was done to prevent a new buildup of debts is not quite clear. Little reliable information remains on Solon's complete legislation. In any case, it did not include land reform, which would have been far too radical for the era. Solon wanted to be a mediator, "a boundary stone between the parties," as he put it, a lawgiver who rectified abuses while retaining the existing order. Poor Athenians probably had to work as laborers from then on, while some may have found work in the newly emerging industries.

In addition to his efforts in the economic field, Solon was active in political reform.

The inside of an Attic black-figured *kylix* (drinking cup), decorated with a picture of a long jumper who holds a weight in each hand in order to get as far as possible

479

Black-figured Attic
amphora (dating from the end
of the sixth or the beginning
of the fifth century BC)
depicting a cobbler
in his shop

grain. There were four groups. In addition to the thetes, zeugitai, and hippeis (defined above), a new group, the *pentakosiomedimnoi* (five hundred medimners), was formed. It comprised men with an income of more than 500 *medimnoi* (roughly 1,500 cubic feet or 420 hectoliters) of grain, or the equivalent. This new class was a group of the superrich detached from the broader group of hippeis. They were granted the honor of performing duties connected with the guardianship of the temple of the goddess Athena. Only they and the hippeis could be elected to the position of archon.

All Athenians had the opportunity to appeal decisions made by the magistrates. For this, Solon turned the public assembly into the highest court of justice. A separate people's court and a Council of 400 existing alongside the areopagus were also attributed to Solon, although these were most likely from a later date.

Solon's reforms did not produce radical changes, although they did achieve their goal, which was to cautiously make social justice a cornerstone of the Athenian state. The rich and privileged had to make sacrifices. Solon described the contents of his reforms as follows: "I gave the people the necessary power—without giving them too much honor; and I took away the excess power from the nobility—without offending their noble feelings unnecessarily. In this way the people follow their leaders without the leaders holding the reins too tightly or too loosely. . . ."

Solon's measures temporarily endorsed the dominance of the aristocracy while allowing the lower classes to become more involved in politics. The new property criteria made social advancement easier, an important social change. This meant that it was no longer necessary to be descended from the nobility to enjoy upperclass privileges; high income was sufficient. The aristocratic structure was, in fact, replaced by a timocratic structure some time after Solon. Timocracy was defined by Aristotle to mean a state in which political power is in direct proportion to property ownership.

He decreed that all free citizens of Attica be allowed to vote in the public assembly, the *ecclesia*. This may have been already the case for most of them, but it is not clear whether the *thetes* (small farmers, day laborers, the landless) in particular had access to the assembly before Solon's reforms. Afterward, they definitely did.

Other political rights were linked to a division of the citizens into classes. These classes were defined by Solon according to a new criterion based solely on property. (Birth had previously been the most important factor.) The classification was based on annual income expressed in terms of quantities of

Young man putting on a cloak. Detail of a *kylix* (drinking cup), dating from the sixth century BC

The Greek Tyrants

Absolute Rulers in a Changing World

During the Archaic period, colonization relieved the pressure of a growing population on the limited resources of the *metropoleis* (mother cities). Legislation was used to resolve other social problems within the daughter *poleis* (city-states). There were attempts, most notably by Solon in Athens in the sixth century BC, to moderate the gaping differences between rich and poor, with Solon specifically addressing the rights of the poor by abolishing debt slavery. A third way of dealing with internal social problems in the Greek communities was the institution of tyranny.

The word *tyrannos* was not originally Greek, but a term borrowed from the Lydian language of Asia Minor. It was used to indicate an absolute ruler who had taken power

Hunting scene,
painted on an Attic vase
from the sixth
century BC

illegally. This was not always a "tyrant" in the conventional sense of the word, since an unlawful sovereign is not necessarily a cruel and unjust ruler. The fact that the Greeks adopted a foreign word for this political phenomenon illustrates that they viewed it as alien to the concept of a polis as a community of citizens.

While noble gentlemen battled each other amid social unrest, individual aristocrats saw their opportunity and seized power all over Greece in the Archaic period. Labeled tyrants in their separate city-states, they alienated the rest of the nobility. In most cases the details of the ascent to power are unknown, but the sparse information available shows signs of military coups. They evidently received support from aristocratic friends and followers, often from another state, as well as from mercenaries, appearing as a new phenomenon in this period. The tyrants also appealed to certain segments of the populace, promising various rewards, including land, and turning social discontent to their own advantage.

One of the first to found a *tyrannis*, or tyranny, was Cypselus, who drove out the ruling aristocracy in Corinth around 650 BC. Over the next one hundred fifty years, tyranny became the most common form of government in the Greek world, particularly in the more important poleis. Only Sparta and Aegina appear to have escaped it. The various tyrannies were not established at the same time, neither did they endure for the same length of time. Most of them lasted for several decades, and many of the tyrants were quite popular, especially among nonaristocratic citizens from whom tyrants were able to canvass support against their own aristocratic rivals. Some tyrants stimulated local patriotism and organized cults and festivals based on "national" principles.

The tyrannies followed a similar pattern in each state. Eventually, popular aversion to the monocratic administration would develop, as councils and tribal meetings were excluded from power and the tyrant placed himself outside the law. Most tyrants decreed their rule hereditary.

Aristocrats and common people tended to unite against the second or third generation of tyrants. As resistance against a given tyrant increased, he would typically take harsh measures in an attempt to remain in power as long as possible. This would incite further resistance and the eventual ousting of the tyrant.

By undermining the position of the aristocracy, the phenomenon of the archaic tyrannis ultimately paved the way for democracy.

The Tyranny in Corinth

After around 750 BC, Corinth, situated on the south of the isthmus joining central Greece to the Peloponnisos, became the most important harbor and the most prosperous city in Greece. Many ships avoided the dangerous journey around the Peloponnisos peninsula. Goods were often transferred to other ships or to smaller boats that were pulled over the isthmus. (The Corinth Canal was dug across the isthmus at this point in AD 1893. Allowing passage through the narrow neck of land, it makes the Peloponnisos an island.) Trade with the east thrived and increased in the west, as well, after the colonization of southern Italy and Sicily in which Corinth played a large part.

Corinth developed its own export industry in earthenware. Corinthian pottery, exemplifying the archaic Orientalizing of art, was shipped out in large quantities to destinations lying in every direction. The Bacchiad family was behind much of the commercial activity. An aristocratic family, it ruled over Corinth in almost regal fashion.

The wealthy Cypselus, relying on popular resentment of the Bacchiadae, seized power and ousted the family. According to a legend later popular in the city, Labda, the mother of Cypselus, was a Bacchiad rejected by her family because of a handicap. She married a stranger, Eetion, and bore him a son. Oracles prophesied that he would grow up to destroy the ruling dynasty. The Bacchiadae attempted to kill the child, but Labda hid him in a chest, called a *kypselē* in Greek; hence the name Cypselus. The boy grew up outside Corinth until another oracle ordered him to return to the city and take control. He complied. The tale is similar to other legends explaining the arrival of a new ruler.

View of Corinth; in the background the Akrokorinth, the impressive *acropolis* (stronghold) of ancient Corinth, can be seen.

Gold coin
from Ephesus
(ca. 600 BC)

The ruins of the temple
of Apollo in Corinth.
It was built in Doric style
around 500 BC
and is therefore one of the most
ancient surviving temples
of Greece.

cuted. Chief among them was a slipway for ships crossing the isthmus, built in roughly the same place as the present Corinthian canal. The tyrants founded colonies on the western edge of the Mediterranean. They appear to have been trading posts dependent on Corinth rather than independent poleis.

An anecdote by the fifth-century historian Herodotus describes the downfall of this tyrannical family:

"At a certain moment Periander sent an envoy to the tyrant Thrasybulus of Miletus to ask him the best way to rule without conflict. Thrasybulus wandered through a cornfield with the envoy, while questioning him about the situation in Corinth. Now and then the tyrant stopped to cut off the largest ears of corn which rose above the others. In this way he destroyed the best of the corn, and he subsequently sent the envoy away without having given an answer. When the envoy returned to Corinth, Periander asked him impatiently what Thrasybulus had advised. The envoy replied truthfully that he had received no answer. He expressed surprise that Periander had sent him to a man who had nothing better to do than destroy the best part of his crop. But Periander understood immediately what Thrasybulus had meant by this action. Believing that this represented the punishment of the most important citizens of Corinth, from that moment he treated the aristocrats and the rich with extreme cruelty. Whereas Cypselus had granted forgiveness and had neither killed nor banished anybody, Periander acted extremely cruelly."

The story shows the deterioration of a tyranny into a reign of terror. Periander was succeeded by his nephew Psammetichus. The fact that he was named after the Pharaoh Psammetichus illustrates the trade links between Corinth and Egypt. Psammetichus was deposed following a rebellion in the third year of his reign. A few aristocrats took over the government, establishing an *oligarchy* (rule by an elite few) in Corinth.

The Tyranny in Athens

Although the actions of Solon in Athens were the first steps toward democracy there, the city experienced an authoritarian regime before any further such development was seen. Solon granted civil rights to the poorer Athenians and ended debt slavery but he did little to ensure their economic future. Rivalry

Cypselus is presented as a hero favored by the gods and as someone who belongs to the same class as the ruling aristocracy, but is an outsider. This seems to be a highly realistic description of the tyrant.

Under the rule of Cypselus and his successor Periander, the "affluence politics" of Corinth continued. Export of Corinthian industrial products remained high. Major public works aimed at encouraging the development of trade in Corinth were exe-

Attic red-figured vase with a picture of a torch race. This type of relay race, in which the torch must be passed on (as visible on the left), was sometimes part of religious festivals.

between landed and landless people continued, as did rivalry within the aristocracy. Herodotus describes the situation that ensued:

"In that time a civil war was raging in Attica between the coastal party, led by Megacles from the Alcmaeonides family, and the plains party, under the command of Lycurgus from the Aristolaides family. Taking advantage of their quarrel, Peisistratus devised a plan to become tyrant of Athens by forming a third party. This was the party from over the hills. He mobilized a group of followers and he managed to win a victory as their leader by means of a clever trick. One day he wounded himself and his mules before coming to the market. There, he said that he had miraculously managed to escape from his enemies, who had wanted to kill him. In order to protect himself from new attacks, he asked for an official bodyguard. . . . The Athenians gave him permission to arm a group of 300 citizens with clubs. . . . With the aid of these people Peisistratus rebelled and succeeded in capturing first the Acropolis and subsequently the seat of government. But he did not change the laws as a tyrant, and he ruled according to traditional customs in a correct and just manner."

There has been considerable speculation as to what was meant by the terms *plains party, coastal party,* and *party from over the hills.* The men of the plains appear to have been the old established aristocratic families from the region surrounding the city of Athens. The coastal party would therefore have been rival families, the most important

The so-called
Françoise Vase
(after its excavator),
a black-figured Attic *krater*
(vessel in which water
and wine was mixed). It was
made between 575 and
555 BC by the potter Ergotimos
and the painter Kleitias,
who painted all sorts
of mythological images on its
surface. This is one of the
earliest examples of
black-figured pottery.

Peisistratus's power base lay on the east coast of Attica, on the other side of the Hymettos Mountain ridge as seen from Athens. Herodotus's account of the coup is not improbable. Peisistratus could have managed to take over the government center by force of arms. His subsequent methods of government strongly resembled those of other benign tyrants who respected existing laws.

Soon after Peisistratus had established himself as a tyrant in 561 BC, he was driven out again by the two rival groups of aristocrats. He returned from exile five years later. As Herodotus tells it:

"As soon as Peisistratus had left, the two groups who had banished him began to quarrel again. Finally Megacles, the leader of the coastal party, sent an envoy to Peisistratus. Peisistratus would be returned to power if he agreed to marry the daughter of Megacles. Peisistratus accepted the proposal and together they designed a plan to accomplish the return of the tyrant."

Herodotus claims that Megacles and Peisistratus succeeded in their plan, thanks to the credulity of the Athenians. The men dressed a statuesque woman as the goddess Pallas Athena. This woman traveled through the city, preceded by heralds who announced that the goddess was leading Peisistratus into the city.

Both the alliance with the coastal party and the marriage with the daughter of Megacles subsequently broke down, and Peisistratus and his family once again had to leave Athens. During the next decade, Peisistratus was active all over the Aegean

of whom were the Alcmaeonides. Solon was probably a member of this family. Their domain lay along the coast to the south of Athens. Peisistratus was related to Solon, and his party from over the hills was probably a splinter group from the coastal party. It was perhaps called "over the hills" because

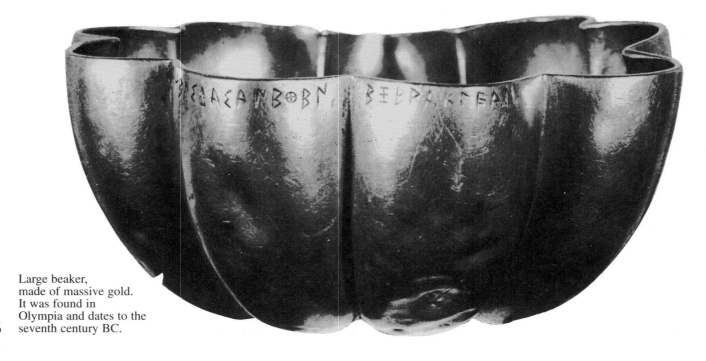

Large beaker,
made of massive gold.
It was found in
Olympia and dates to the
seventh century BC.

region. First he concentrated on accumulating wealth, earning a great deal from gold and silver mines in Thrace. He then established relations with states and individuals prepared to supply funds and mercenaries in support of his planned coup in Athens. In 546 BC, he landed an army in Marathon on the east coast of Attica. Joined by followers from Attica, he defeated his opponents in battle, sending them into exile. Peisistratus remained absolute ruler until his death about 528 BC, whereupon he was succeeded by his two sons, Hippias and Hipparchus. Athens flourished under all three, although it is not always possible to distinguish the separate elements of their reigns.

In matters of foreign policy, Athens functioned as the center of the Ionian Greeks. Internally, policy concentrated on the avoidance of drastic breaks with the past. Existing laws were maintained and existing administrative structures remained intact. Archons were elected each year. In some instances, they even included members of rival families, back from exile and reconciled to the situation. Efforts were made to reinforce the position of the city of Athens as the political center for the whole of Attica, mainly organizing through "national" religious festivities. Dionysian festivals were organized, notably the Great Dionysia where tragedies were performed. The Panathenaea, the celebration of the city goddess Athena, was turned into another festival. The verses of Homer were recited here, among other events. Construction projects were included in the campaign to emphasize the great importance to Attica of Athens and the ruling family. Poorer Athenians seem to have benefited under the Peisistratids from a redistribution of land and a stimulation of industry and trade. The pottery industry, in particular, flourished. Athenian black-figure pottery and the more modern red-figure pottery dating from 550 BC soon superseded all other pottery on the Mediterranean export markets.

About 514 BC, two men, Harmodius and Aristogeiton, decided to dispose of the sons of Peisistratus for personal reasons. They

Hunters and their dogs catch a wild boar. Corinthian *aryballos* (oil flask) made in the sixth century BC

only succeeded in killing one of them, Hipparchus. Harmodius was killed in the process by the bodyguard of the tyrants, while Aristogeiton was later tortured to death. Hippias went on to rule with great severity after the assault, but this only served to accelerate his own end.

The powerful family of the Alcmaeonides had gathered together a large group of exiles on the Peloponnisos. They managed to gain the support of the Spartans, who were unsuccessfully trying to expand their territory north. A Spartan army joined an invasion of Attica in 510 BC. Hippias was surrounded and forced to surrender. He subsequently left for a colony in the Dardanelles. The Athenian tyranny had ended. Harmodius and Aristogeiton, declared "tyrant killers," were seen as the heroes of democratic Athens. The aristocrats were once again in control but they would soon be forced to make major political concessions to the rest of the Athenian people.

Economic Life in Ancient Times

Cypselus and Peisistratus alike appear to

Vomiting man,
depicted on an Athenian
wine cup from the
fifth century BC

The remains of the
temple of Poseidon in Cape
Sunion (Attica).
The building was erected
in the fifth century BC.

have gained great personal wealth and to have boosted industry and export during their respective reigns. Both handicrafts and trade were important features of economic life in the Greek world, but the economic center of gravity lay in agriculture.

Agriculture was the basis of the economy throughout the ancient world. Some 90 percent of the population worked in this sector. In fundamental contrast to the modern industrial society, handicrafts, trade, and services were always relatively marginal in ancient

489

times. Agricultural methods were primitive and underwent no great change for millennia. Work on the land was carried out by individual farmer-landholders or by dependent tenant farmers or serfs. Most Greek farms were small, although there were occa-

Ruins of the *Telesterion* (mystery temple) at Eleusis. Here, Demeter was worshiped as the goddess of the grain, who was supposed to make new crops grow on the fields each year.

sional large holdings. The ideal of the citizens was landownership (preferably a lot of land), on which the traditional farming methods of one's fathers could be practiced (preferably by someone else). Wealth was primarily expressed in terms of land. Agriculture had an effect, even on urban values.

Industrial production in Greece during the Archaic period was just as small-scale as agricultural production. Potters, smiths, tanners, and other craftsmen generally worked in small workshops, usually in a family business. Textile production was a domestic industry carried out by women. Only a small handful of people in each polis could have survived by doing nonagricultural work. Craftsmen were not held in high esteem. According to the fourth-century Athenian author Xenophon, "Craftsmanship has a bad name and is quite rightly greatly despised. . . . . It makes such demands on a man that he can no longer devote himself to his friends or to the polis. Such people must be bad friends and bad defenders of their nation. . . . The best occupations are farming and the waging of war."

It is difficult to imagine that the average Greek craftsman viewed his work so negatively, but work was equated with a lack of freedom. The work of the farmer was rated more highly than the work of the "wage slave," dependent on his employer, or the work of the small craftsman or trader, dependent on customers. The farmer was considered to have the greatest personal freedom.

Trade in Greece was carried out by farmers who brought their surplus to the market and by craftsmen who served their customers in the workshop. Professional traders, people who bought the products of others in order to resell them at a profit, were rare in Archaic Greece. The Greek overseas trade in that era was in the hands of prosperous people able to build and equip a ship. These people did not undertake the trading voyages themselves, but left that to others.

The colonization efforts of the Greeks definitely boosted the overseas trade between motherland and colonies, but a lack of data makes it difficult to estimate the contribution of this trade to the total economy. Before 500 BC, the volume of exports and imports would have been considerably lower in the Greek world than in Mesopotamia or Phoenicia.

War was another important economic factor in ancient times. The booty taken on military enterprises often provided a direct source of wealth. With wars waged almost constantly among the numerous Greek poleis, war booty was probably the major source of income other than agricultural pro-

Statue of Harmodius and Aristogeiton, who murdered Hipparchos in 514 BC. The victim was the son and successor of the tyrant Peisistratus. Therefore, the two muderers are depicted here as heroic tyrant killers.

duction. The link between war and economy is demonstrated by the fact that the very first coins were, in all probability, intended to pay mercenaries. These were minted in the seventh century by the Lydian kings of Asia Minor. Pieces of electrum, a natural alloy of gold and silver, were stamped on one side with a mark, which guaranteed their weight and thus their value. Greek adventurers acting as mercenaries were also paid with these coins. Around 600 BC, Greek cities on the coast of Asia Minor, notably Ephesus and Miletus, began to mint their own coins. These were silver, marked with the stamp of the polis. In the course of the sixth century, Greek states in Europe also adopted this custom. During the Athenian tyranny, the owl, representing the goddess Athena, was used as an emblem. In Lydia, the use of coins remained limited in the sixth century, but in Greece it had acquired great importance. By that time, small bronze coins were minted and circulated, undoubtedly helping to boost trade, both local and international. However, the introduction of coinage did not create a full monetary economy. Bartering always retained a predominant role.

However small-scale or marginal, trade in the Archaic period offered unprecedented opportunities for enrichment. The social advancement of large groups of the populace due to a general rise in prosperity, in addition to the great riches acquired by some individuals, led to the social turmoil which manifested itself in tyranny. These changes taking place in his world are expressed by the conservative poet Theognis, who writes halfway through the sixth century, "Wealth, the people do not revere you for nothing! For you overlook their evil. It would be better if only the good were rich and if poverty were the companion of all inferior people."

Reality would continue to diverge from Theognis's ideal.

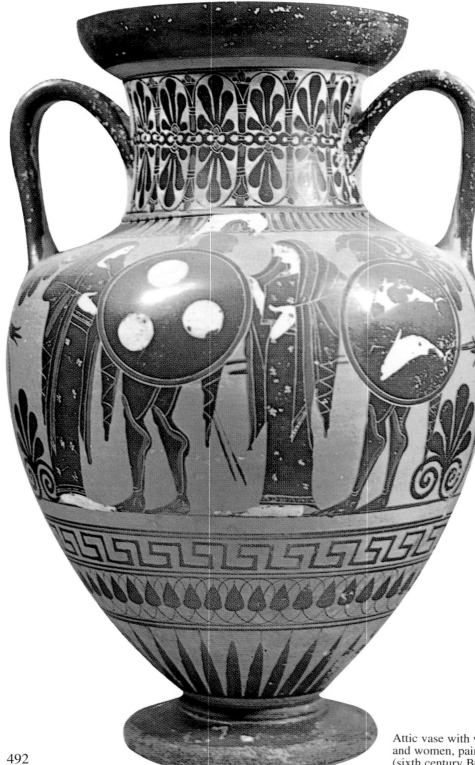

Attic vase with warriors and women, painted by Antimenes (sixth century BC)

Votive relief. On the left, a family dedicates a sow to Demeter and Persephone, who are standing to their right. The difference in height between ordinary mortals and the goddesses is striking.

Greek Religion

Ideas about the World and Its Surroundings

Although religious life differed from polis to polis, literature gives us insights into "the" Greek religion. *Theogony* (*Genealogy of the Gods*) is by the poet Hesiod. Homer is credited with authorship of the *Homeric Hymns*, short poetic celebrations of the many Greek gods. There was no theological dogma, or teaching.

In the *Theogony*, Hesiod compiles the vast collection of Greek myths into systematic form, including deities not described by Homer. He details the creation of the world, the origin of the gods and anecdotes about them, listing the daughters of Zeus.

The Greeks had no form of written scripture and made no claim to sacred revelation. Their religion was polytheistic. They imagined the gods as supernatural beings living in

ΔΙΟΝΥΣΟΣ ΑΜΑΣΙΣ ΜΕΠΟΙΕΣΕΝ

Dionysus, the god
of wine and drunkenness,
who is carrying a *kantharos*
(vessel) is offered a hare
and a little stag by two Maenads
(devotees of Dionysus).
Cup from ca. 530 BC

their own hierarchy. Most deities were portrayed anthropomorphically, or in human form.

There were heroes (including "demigods," or deified mortals) and spirits of various nature, both good and evil. There were also a number of odd creatures of myth, often seen with Dionysus, the very popular god of wine and pleasure. They included satyrs that had goat legs and the upper body of a monkey or human, centaurs with the head and torso of a man and the body of a horse, and nymphs, lovely females of the forests.

In practice, this polytheism created uncertainty as to which divine power to address with a particular concern. The Greeks consulted seers and oracles for answers. An oracle could be any medium by which the gods were consulted, including a place or a person. There was no set doctrine to follow. Greek priests and priestesses existed but,

with a few exceptions, there was no caste of professional priests with a special status. Priests and priestesses were often chosen or drawn by lot for a set period of time.

Greek religious life comprised a number of rituals and celebrations, often shared by the entire community. Each city had its own god (or gods) with temples dedicated to a god. There was a vast repertoire of sacrifices, prayers to the gods, music and dance, processions, and competitions for singers or reciters of poetry, dancers, musicians, dramatists, and athletes. The goal was to pla-

The remains of Olympia, where the ❯
most important sanctuary of the Greek
supreme god Zeus stood. This was also the
location of the Olympic Games, held in
Zeus's honor once every four years.

Actaeon has been spying on Artemis while she is taking a bath, and she changes him into a deer so that his own dogs tear him to pieces. Relief on the temple of Hera in Selinus, a Greek colony on Sicily, dating from around 460 BC

Attic red-figured *pelikē* (type of amphora), depicting Ganymede pouring some wine for Zeus

cate the gods, not to look to them for spiritual guidance in daily life. Sacrifices were considered the most important element of worship. Animals, usually goats, were sacrificed (ritually killed) for "bloody offerings" at an altar, usually outside, in front of a temple. The sacrificed animal was sometimes totally cremated, but more often the gods were considered satisfied with only the aroma of the shanks. All the other meat was eaten during the feast that followed the offering. Non-bloody offerings could include the burning or placing of food on the altar, libations of wine, milk, olive oil, or aromatics, or the burning of incense. Worshipers offered the gods samplings of the best that they had in order to express gratitude or to honor them, or because they sought something from the deities in return. People often requested the god to give something first, promising to bring an offering if this or that happened.

Votive offerings included land, slaves, cattle, money, and valuables such as weapons, textiles, jewels, or objects of art.

The gods were worshiped at home as well as in public. Every home had altars appropriate to the god's function around the house (the goddess of the hearth was Hestia, for example). Humans were seen as insignificant before the vast forces of nature the gods represented. All people could do was to try to please the gods through prayer and offerings. The gods did not look favorably on *hubris* (exaggerated pride) or an excess of ambition or wealth.

The Origins of the Greek Religion

The Mycenaean Linear B tablets mention various gods who are members of the later Greek divine family, such as Zeus, Hera, Poseidon, Dionysus, and Hermes, but also mention other divine figures apparently for-

496

gotten after the Mycenaean epoch. Little or no association can be found between the evidence of the Linear B tablets and archaeological finds. Of all the presumed goddesses portrayed on frescoes, for example, none can be identified as Hera. It is interesting to note that male gods are prevalent in the texts, while in the archaeological material, goddesses appear to be favored.

Architectural evidence may offer clues to religious connections. For instance, there is a similarity in form between the Mycenaean *megaron* (square) and the later Greek temple, but it is difficult to establish a direct link between them.

A major question is whether the divine family already existed before the first Greek-speaking peoples entered Greece. Father Zeus, Zeus pater, seems to be the counterpart of Dyaus Pitar, god of the heavens of the Indo-European peoples in India. He may also be recognized as Diespiter, or the Roman Jupiter. This is the universal divine father figure who was worshiped by the Indo-European-speaking people from India to western Europe. Helios, the sun god, and Eos Aurora, the goddess of dawn, can likewise be considered of Indo-European heritage, as can certain aspects of sacrifice and prayer.

Although certain gods were already worshiped during the Bronze Age and certain customs can be presumed to be ages-old, it is difficult to discern much continuity between the Bronze Age and the later Dark Age. Only a few of the Dark Age sanctuaries had Bronze Age predecessors. Even in those cases, a clear break can be seen at the end of the Bronze Age. The earlier custom of making religious sculpture, for example, seems to disappear entirely in the later era. But we can say with certainty that during the Dark Age, Greek religion underwent major changes, while this period also marks the actual beginning of Greek religion as we know it.

This complex world of multiple gods, a variety of mythological tales, and religious rituals surely had roots in many soils. Various influences have contributed to it: Indo-European heritage via the Greek Mycenaeans, the Greek-speaking people who came to the region after them; pre-

Painted terra-cotta statue (made in Attica) of a shepherd carrying a lamb in his arms

497

Ruins of a *tholos* (round building) in the sanctuary of Athena in Delphi. It was built in the fourth century BC and used to have a dome-shaped roof. The function of this building is unknown.

Painted terra-cotta statuette from Tanagra, Boeotia, possibly portraying the goddess Demeter or Persephone (around 575 BC)

Greek elements, Minoan or others; and influence from Anatolia and from Syrian regions, often via Cyprus. The god Apollo exhibits all these influences.

Apollo is the paramount god of the Dorian people. The name *Apollo* may be related to the name of the Dorian public meetings, the apella. As the god of music and dance, on the other hand, Apollo seems to have Minoan antecedents, while Apollo the archer, the god who brings disease with his arrows (but also cures them), may have Semitic and partly Hittite connections. In some cases, the influences from the east are very strong: the goddess Aphrodite is none other than the Phoenician Astarte, who is in turn related to the Babylonian Ishtar. This is yet another illustration of the great cultural influence from the east, a factor often pushed into the background in order to highlight the uniqueness and originality of Greek civilization.

Oracles and Mysteries

From the eighth century on, certain sanctuaries associated with oracles or mystery cults were honored everywhere and widely considered holy. Priests, sometimes local officials, were present at each such site to offer interpretation of the oracle or prophecy, but they did not have any particular training for this and were not considered to have any unusual power. These places were subject to outside influence from adjacent regions and even from other nations. In the world of oracles, Oriental and Egyptian examples are apparent. They seem to have made their influence in Greece at an early stage. The *Iliad* mentions an oracle of Zeus in Dodona, in northern Greece. The most famous example is the oracle of Delphi, a sanctuary to Apollo on the top of Mount Parnassus. The notion that the priestess, called *pythia*, became intoxicated by volcanic gases arising from a crevice, is relegated to the realm of fiction by geologists. The pythia probably fell into a trance through her own powers; priests then translated her mumblings into understandable language. These did not predict the future, but helped in making decisions, often on religious questions. One of the first applications of the alphabet writings in the Greek world was the recording of oracular utterings. Many of the oracular sayings of Delphi and other oracles that have

Attic funerary relief, dating from the end of the fifth century BC. Zeus is sitting on the left; the people next to him are probably his wife Hera and the god Apollo. The much smaller person on the right is the deceased.

been passed down were written to support a certain policy, or simply made up as a good story.

Besides oracles, Greek mysteries began to play a role between the seventh and the sixth centuries BC, even though their roots are much older. The religion of the polis community was very public; ceremonies and celebrations were for the entire community. The mysteries, on the other hand, consisted of secret rituals devoted to initiating the worshipers. The purpose was to liberate the initiates from their earthly bonds and shortcomings and to show the way to a happy life after death, in another world. The problem with the interpretation of this mystery world is the

499

An uncarved chunk of rock in the sanctuary of Apollo in Delphi. The stone is what remains of a still older sanctuary of the goddess Gaea-Themis, and was later known as "the Sybil's seat."

The most famous Greek mysteries were those at Eleusis, on the coast near Athens. During the millennium from 600 BC to AD 400, people gathered together to become initiated. The subject of the Eleusinian mysteries was the legend of Persephone, who was abducted by Hades and brought to the underworld. She was later saved by her mother Demeter, at least for part of the year. The initiation ceremonies had a fixed date on the calendar: the autumn month of Budromion. The main public event was a procession from Athens to Eleusis, some twenty-five miles (40 kilometers) over the "Holy Road." The arrival was followed by the initiation in the *Telesterion* (initiation building), where the people could see everything. Those who attended this ceremony left it with the expectation of a better fate in the hereafter.

Religion and Philosophy

The average Greek worshiper took part in the rituals of his community, accepted the existence of all sorts of supernatural powers, consulted an oracle once in a while, and was initiated at least once in a mystery cult. The flexibility of the Greek religion generally offered sufficient room for most people, but not all. Some individuals had difficulty accepting the widespread *pluriformity* (many forms) of the gods. For example, Aphrodite was considered to have very different images in various poleis. There was also the old problem of *theodicy*, the moral dilemma that good is not always rewarded, and evil not always punished.

fact that "secret" in this case really means secret. We have no reliable sources as to what exactly happened during these mystery rituals.

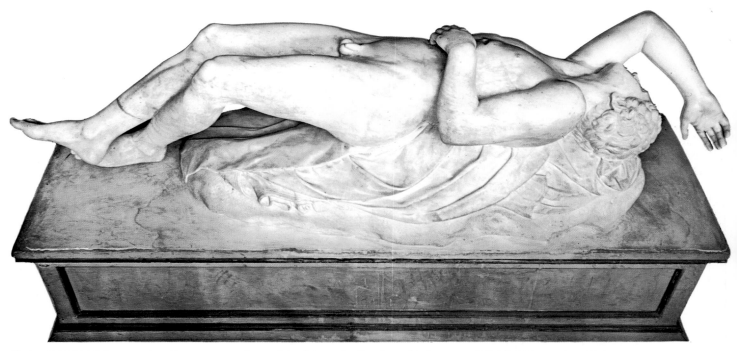

Dying Niobid. This statue is a Roman copy of an original from the fourth or third century BC. Niobids are the children of Niobe, who boasted to Leto (Apollo's and Artemis's mother) about the great number of children she had. This meant their destruction: Apollo and Artemis killed all of her twelve children, whereupon Niobe herself turned into stone with grief.

The Olympic Gods

The peoples of ancient Asia Minor used to consider their main gods as belonging to a family of twelve. The ancient Greeks adopted this, and soon had their own "family of gods": Zeus, Hera, Poseidon, Athena, Apollo, Artemis, Aphrodite, Hermes, Demeter, Dionysus, Hephaistus, and Ares. These gods lived together as a family on the sacred Mount Olympus. Zeus and Poseidon are brothers: Zeus is the lord of the skies, Poseidon is the lord of the waters, and together they rule the land. The third brother is Hades, the lord of the underworld, who does not belong to the Olympus. Hera is the sister and the wife of Zeus, and mainly serves as goddess of marriage. Athena is Zeus' daughter: she was born out of his head, without having a mother. Athena is a virgin goddess, and has a series of different functions. She appears as a war goddess, but is also potectress of women's domestic handwork. Apollo and Artemis are the chlidren of Zeus whom he has begotten by Leto. Apollo is the god of oracles, he brings sickness and health, and is also the god of the music arts: he is the leader of the nine Muses. Artemis, another virgin goddess, is the mistress of all wild animals. She is the goddess of nature, hunting, and of the initiation of young girls (the idea being that the young virgin is still "wild," and still belongs to free nature, whereas only the married woman and mother belongs to the civilized world). Aphrodite is the goddess of love and sexuality, who was born from the sea. Hermes, the son of Zeus and Maia, is the messenger of the gods, and also the protector of shepherds, thieves, and heralds. Hermes also guides the souls of the deceased to the underworld. The mysterious Demeter, sister of Zeus, Poseidon and Hades, is the goddess of agriculture and therefore, generally speaking, of fertility. Dionysus, son of Zeus and Semele, is the god of wine and ecstasy, but also of madness and death. Hephaistus, son of Zeus and Hera, is the smith-god, the able craftsman. He is the outsider of the family, and is always depicted as a cripple. Aphrodite is considered to be his wife. Ares, also a son of Zeus and Hera, is the somewhat marginal god of war, and often Athena's adversary. Apart from his role on the battlefields, he also acts as Aphrodite's lover. The fact that there have never been orthodox principles in Greek religion leads to the conclusion that there is no uniformity in Greek mythology: in the stories that have been transmitted from ancient times it sometimes happens that the family of gods is different than the list given above. Also, the various family bonds and the stories about the lives, deeds and relationships of the different gods are told with many variations. The main characteristic of these gods,

however, is their anthropomorphic character: though they are immortal (which of course makes a great difference) they resemble human beings very much, both in their outer appearance and in their defects. These human characteristics of the gods were not appreciated by all ancient Greeks. Therefore, several Greek thinkers and philosophers opted for a different approach. They preferred to worship a higher and more ideal godly image, which of course made the colorful family living on Olympus superfluous.

Zeus and Hera on a relief in the temple of Hera in Selinus (Sicily). It dates from around 460 BC.

Detail of a terra-cotta frieze from Italy (first or second century AD). It depicts an initiation in the so-called Small Mysteries. Demeter is sitting on the left, holding a torch. The person in front of her is extending his hand toward the snake on her lap.

The solutions the Greek thinkers postulated ranged from *henotheism,* the idea that one god is more important than the other gods, to *monotheism*, the idea that there is only one god, to *atheism*, the idea that no god exists at all. The development of such opinions forms a part of a wider secularization process. For example, the famous fifth-century BC physician Hippocrates searched for a natural rather than supernatural explanation for disease. The historian Thucydides made no allowance for divine intervention in the course of history, and the philosopher Protagoras, also of the fifth century, claimed that all knowledge is relative, expressed in

Bust of the Greek poet Hesiod, among whose surviving works is the *Theogony*, a narrative poem about the origins and exploits of the gods. He lived around 700 BC.

his famous saying, "Man is the measure of all things." Even when people did not go so far as to doubt the existence of the gods, the relationship between the godhead, fate, and man's own responsibility became a central theme during the fifth and fourth centuries BC. The history of Greek philosophy can offer some understanding of these debates.

Ionian Philosophy

During the sixth century BC in Ionia, a number of people sought a different explanation of the origins of heaven and earth than the ones offered by traditional cosmologies. Located in Asia Minor, Ionia was part of a region where people were more informed about other lands and cultures than people elsewhere in Greece. They were able to share in such intellectual accomplishments of other cultures as the discoveries of Babylonian astronomers. This may have been why they did not think in traditional ways. They could usually discuss and analyze the phenomena around them without opposition from officialdom. Thus, philosophy and natural science were born, though initially not as separate fields.

Later modern scholars of Greek philosophy spoke of "natural philosophers" or "pre-Socratics," to indicate those sixth- and fifth-centuries BC thinkers who tried to describe and explain the origin and existence of the cosmos in a rational manner, without appealing to religion or mythology. They were searching for one basic principle that could explain the entire cosmos.

The first great scholar of this rank that we know of was Thales of Miletus (in Ionia), considered the founder of Greek philosophy. At some time in the first half of the sixth century, he rejected a mythological explanation of the universe. We know of Thales, who was noted for his knowledge of astronomy, from Aristotle's *Metaphysics*; he left no writings. It is possible that he did indeed predict, as reputed, the solar eclipse of May 28, 585 BC. It is important to recognize that Thales took the trouble to calculate it using Babylonian techniques, reaching for mathematical knowledge from the east, perhaps also from Egypt. He is said to have introduced geometry into the Greek world, utilizing Egyptian examples and applications. It is his focus on the physical substance basic to the world, however, that allows Thales to be called the first scientist. His work is regarded as the first real scientific inquiry. He postulated that the original principle of the cosmos is water, from which everything proceeds and into which everything is again resolved.

Thales's pupil, Anaximander of Miletus, is said to have been the first Greek to have made a world map and a sundial, introducing a number of hypotheses concerning astronomy, as well. A striking theory about the development of life on earth, from fish to land animals, and finally to humans, is further attributed to him. His philosophic position is fairly certain, although all but one

sentence of his writings *About Nature* have been lost. According to Anaximander, the entire cosmos was created and derived from something that he called "the indeterminate" or "the unlimited." Everything originated from this imperishable stuff he called protoplasm, which he defined as the first element formed. After perishing, everything would return to this same protoplasm. As he saw it, there were other worlds that came and went.

A student of Anaximander, Anaximenes of Miletus, continued the work of the Ionian school in the second half of the sixth century

The Erechtheum on the Acropolis of Athens. The olive tree in the foreground is exactly on the spot where, according to tradition, Pallas Athena planted the first olive tree as a gift to the Athenian citizens.

503

Bust of Thales of Miletus, the earliest known Ionian natural philosopher

BC. The last of the three great scholars of the School of Miletus, Anaximenes set up a natural philosophy system based on the principle that a different protoplasm was the origin of all things and beings (including the gods). This primary element was air. Air, he pointed out, could be condensed into water and, further, into earth or could be rarified into fire. Anaximenes was thus able to derive the four elements (earth, water, air, and fire) he saw as basic to nature from one principle. He compared the nature of man to that of the world. A sentence has been passed down, though somewhat changed over the years, which sums up his concept: "As the soul, which is breath, holds us together, so does air hold the whole world together."

In addition to the three thinkers of Miletus, Ionian natural philosophy was also represented by Xenophanes and Heraclitus. Xenophanes, a poet-philosopher from Colophon, near Miletus, lived from about 580 to 480 BC. He left his place of birth when it came under Persian rule and settled in the city of Elea in southern Italy. From there he roamed through southern Italy, Sicily, and probably the Greek mainland until old age. Xenophanes did not advance clear-cut teachings. Through poetry, he criticized the opinions of his contemporaries, questioning their anthropomorphic images of gods and mythical explanations of the world. He also challenged the speculations of other philosophers, including Anaximander. He was fierce in his attacks, suggesting at one point that if cows, horses, and lions could draw, they would portray the gods as just like themselves. He also turned against wealth, certain customs in the drinking parties of the nobility, soothsaying, and the idolization of the winners at the Olympic Games. In that last case, he emphasizes that it is better to honor a scholar than an athlete. A learned man can benefit you in the managing of the polis; his wise counsel can even bring you money: "The knowledge that I have far surpasses the power of man or horse." Xenophanes's criticism is based on his conviction that sensory perceptions are always deceptive and that it is consequently not possible to arrive at certain knowledge. Certain knowledge only resides in the divine, an invisible, unknowable, omnipresent god.

Heraclitus of Ephesus, who probably lived from about 560 to 480 BC, postulated a single explanatory principle (logos), through which the entire cosmos is organized and directed. Opposite entities such as night and day or hot and cold are shown to arise from each other and inhere in each other and have a balanced tension between opposing elements or forces through which the ordered world is produced and maintained. The material embodiment of the logos is fire, which Heraclitus considered to be the essential form of matter. The equilibrium between fire, water, and earth is perpetuated according to the logos, the directing force that ensures that change in one area is balanced by an equivalent and opposite change elsewhere. Heraclitus is best known for the view attributed to him by Plato that "all things are in flux," so that one cannot step into the same river twice.

Ionian natural philosophy began with a scientific study of the macrocosm. But by also involving human nature in their considerations, the great thinkers brought the microcosm of man and the human spirit into the philosophic and scientific fields of inquiry.

Apollo and Heracles are quarreling about a tripod, but Zeus intervenes. Detail of the front of the Siphnian Treasury in Delphi

504

Greek stele from the fifth century BC, depicting a man and a woman playing with a dog.

Cleisthenes

The Creation of the Athenian Democracy

In 510 BC, it was clear to most Athenians that there was still something wrong with their form of government. The statesman and legislator Solon had given citizenship to the lower classes in 594 BC. The tyranny of Peisistratus (560–527 BC), although wise and tolerant, and that of his sons, considerably more despotic, indicated that Solon's reforms were not sufficient. Solon had offered some economic justice, but not economic security. Peisistratus had given Athenians a further taste of political justice.

After these changes, it was impossible to return to the old-style aristocratic regime.

The aristocrat Cleisthenes had been closely involved in the effort to depose Hippias, the surviving son of Peisistratus. (The other son, Hipparchus, had been assassinated in 514 BC.) Cleisthenes saw the opportunity to establish a new democracy based on the political emancipation of the *dēmos*, or Athenian people, that had occurred under Solon and Peisistratus. Cleisthenes sought support among the dèmos. In the words of

Section of the Athenian *agora* (marketplace). In the background is the Hephaesteum (also known as the Theseum), a Doric temple dedicated to the god Hephaestus. This building was erected in the fifth century BC and is now the best-preserved Doric temple.

Attic red-figured *lekythos* (oil flask), decorated with a picture of two women and a wool basket

the fifth-century historian Herodotus, "Cleisthenes added the demos to his group of followers."

The events of the years 510 to 507 BC cannot be reconstructed precisely, but it is known that Cleisthenes instigated a program of political reforms. His new constitution, based on democratic principles, took effect about 502 BC. As a result, the political weight in Athens shifted from the aristocrats to the demos, in particular to the large group of *zeugitai*, the economically independent farmers. (The word stems from *zeugos* or oxen; these farmers had sufficient wealth to own a yoke of oxen.) Under Solon, they had been allowed political office. During the reign of tyranny, many zeugitai had become prosperous enough to be able to afford the full suit of armor required to be a *hoplite* (a foot soldier fighting with the round shield called the *hoplon*). Their role as hoplites became increasingly significant. The importance of these zeugitai to the military security of the polis was certainly a relevant factor in Cleisthenes's decision to approach them for political support.

Under Cleisthenes, Athens saw the beginning of democratic rule. The nucleus of the political reforms was the creation of a new institution, called the *Boulē*, the Council of 500. It became the pivotal point of political

life in Athens, although the ultimate power of decision lay with the tribal meeting and not with the council. The council consisted of ten groups of fifty men each, selected annually through a complex system which ensured that each of the ten groups represented the total polis. The same principle applied to the hoplite army, which was also split into ten subdivisions. The intention was to avoid a situation where all the citizens living in a particular area might jointly form a section of the council or a division of the army. A regional distribution like that would have allowed the most powerful aristocrats in a given geographical area to gain political control of Athens or its army.

Under the new system, the entire Athenian citizenry was split into ten sections, each section representing the polis in miniature. These ten sections were called *phylae*, the basis of the Cleisthenic constitution. To form them, the local communities in Attica were divided into ten urban, ten coastal, and ten rural districts. A district was then taken from each category—one urban, one coastal, and one rural—and the three combined into one *phyle*. The phyle was an artificial unit, its urban, coastal, and rural sections often not even adjoining. It was designed to thoroughly blend the population of Attica in order to prevent the pursuit of local interests. The

ē

resulting body was expected to devote its full attention to general interests. The ten Cleisthenic phylae formed the basis for all democratic institutions in Athens.

Shortly after Cleisthenes initiated his reforms, the practice of ostracism was introduced. Its name comes from *ostracon*, the Greek word for potsherd, or a fragment of broken pottery. Potsherds were used like scrap paper to record votes. The Athenian citizens voted every year in the tribal meeting on the question of political banishment, called ostracism. If it was decided to hold an ostracism, a quorum of 6,000 citizens gathered. Each had to scratch the name of a political leader he wanted banished on a potsherd. Whoever received the most votes had to leave the city for ten years. The aim was to prevent a *tyrannis* and safeguard the young Athenian democracy.

How the Athenian Democracy Worked

The Athenian government was a direct democracy. There was no system of representation by elected delegates in the public assembly, or *ecclesia*, the most important component of polis government. It was a general assembly of all citizens. Other administrative bodies were composed of either the entire citizenry or representatives, who were sometimes elected but were usually appointed by lot.

The ecclesia, where most important political decisions were made, met an estimated ten or eleven times a year in the fifth century. Extra meetings could be convened if exceptional circumstances made it necessary. The Council of 500 exerted great influence on the public assembly because it was primarily responsible for setting the agenda. Outside of subjects like the grain supply, military affairs, and the appointment of magistrates, all of which had to be addressed, the council determined what would be dealt with at each meeting. It could make specific proposals to the ecclesia, but its preliminary agenda was not binding. The public assembly could accept it but could also simply add alternative suggestions or new items for discussion. Because the public assembly had the last word, a powerful council did not pose a threat to the democracy. The fact that the council proposed the agenda was convenient. There was a lot of work to do and holding discussions within its smaller group was more efficient than consulting with the

Relief from the Parthenon with a picture of a centaur snatching a Lapithic woman. The Lapiths were a people from Thessaly; they fought and defeated the centaurs, a race of mythical creatures with a human torso and a horse's hindquarters and legs.

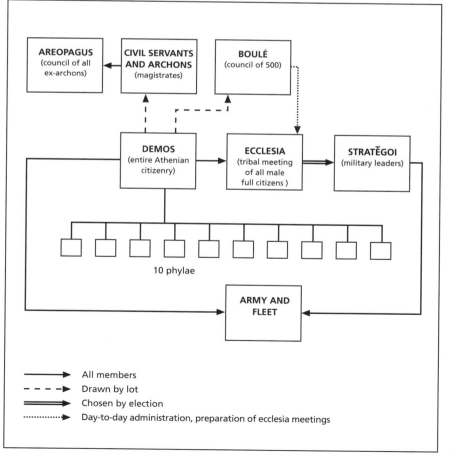

The working of the Athenian democracy

Attic red-figured vase from the fifth century BC, depicting the return of Hephaestus to Olympus. The queue is headed by a satyr playing an *aulos* (double flute); next are a *maenad* (madwoman) and Dionysus, each holding a *kantharos* (beaker) and a *thyrsus* (staff with a pinecone on top, usually carried by the bacchants).

several thousand members of the public assembly. For the same reason, the public assembly was prepared to delegate less important matters and emergency decisions to the council.

The five hundred council members were citizens aged thirty and over who occupied the position for a period of one year, never more than twice in a lifetime. The council members came from all over Attica. This distribution was achieved by taking fifty men from each of the ten phylae. Within the phylae, council members were chosen by lot from a pool of candidates supplied by all villages and urban districts. In small communities, every adult male probably had a chance to be on the council sooner or later, but this was less likely in larger communities.

The council met frequently but was not in permanent session. One of its tasks was to implement decisions made by the public assembly. Since this required an administration available all the time, the prytane system was created. In each of the ten months of the year (the Athenian calendar divided the year into ten months), fifty council members belonging to the same phyle were designated as *prytaneis*, the prytanes. These fifty men formed the daily administration. A smaller group selected from the fifty was ready and available twenty-four hours a day, living

together for this purpose in a building on the Agora. The prytanes prepared, convened, and recessed council and tribal meetings, and received envoys, messengers, complaints, and requests. The Greeks always liked to introduce a competitive element and did so in this case; groups of prytanes competed for the title of "best prytanes of the year."

The prytanes had a different chairman every twenty-four hours, also appointed by lot. A man could only hold this chairmanship once in his lifetime, hereby indicating how far the direct democracy really went. An ordinary man from a small village in Attica had a good chance of becoming chairman of the daily administration. His village had to supply a number of council members each year, and because the number of men aged thirty and above was limited, it was highly probable that he would be selected at least once. Once chosen, he would belong to the prytane administration for a month. With thirty-five or thirty-six days in the Athenian month, he would have a 70 percent chance of being appointed chairman.

In the fifth century BC, the chairman of the prytanes also acted as chairman of the council and of the public assembly if these happened to assemble on that day. He was also in charge of the city seal and the keys to

Attic red-figured *kylix* (drinking cup), dating from around 470 BC and decorated with a picture of two fighting *hoplites* (heavily armed soldiers). Despite their representation here, hoplites did not ordinarily fight in the nude.

the temples, which also functioned as the treasury. It is difficult to imagine how a farmer from a small village might have reacted to such responsibility.

The Limitations of the Athenian Democracy

There were some limitations to the Athenian democracy. Citizens were allowed to participate in direct democracy regardless of their descent and the amount of property they owned, but not everyone living in the polis had civil rights. First of all, women were excluded. This is not surprising; women were excluded from almost all public life in the Greek world, including the political arena. Only male citizens of Attica were called Athenians, after the city of Athens. The polis was called Athens and not Attica, Athens being the political center. The wives of its citizens were never called Athenians, but were called Attic women. Women were considered apolitical beings and had no part in any aspect of city life.

Other criteria for entitlement to civil rights included being free (slaves had no political rights whatsoever), being of Athenian descent (immigrants who settled in Attica could not become citizens), and being adult. Only a relatively few men were full Athenian citizens; democracy was intended for a small minority of the population.

It seems rather improbable that tens of thousands of citizens from all over Attica would have flocked to the city of Athens for the public assembly. Although it was their right to attend, it was not necessarily their

Reliefs from the so-called Tomb of the Harpies (in fact, Sirens) at Xanthus, dating from the early fifth century BC. The Harpies were storm goddesses, and later also tormentresses.

obligation. It does appear that only a small minority of the citizens actually attended the meetings. There was enough room for about six thousand men on the Pnyx, the hill in Athens where the public assembly convened after the end of the sixth century BC. While this is a respectable number for a meeting, it still only represents a small proportion of the population. Six thousand was apparently considered enough to be termed "the entire population of Athens." It was also the number required for a quorum at an ostracism.

Terra-cotta statue
of a woman,
made in Boeotia in the
middle of the fifth
century BC

Evidently not all citizens jostled for a place at the ecclesia, even when extremely important issues were being discussed. Many lived too far away or were unable or unwilling to miss a day's work. Citizens from the city of Athens and the adjacent districts must have constituted the majority at the assemblies.

Implicit here is a relative overrepresentation of the more affluent people, who did not work the land themselves and who lived in the city, and of the poor *thetes* who had no land. Only a small minority of citizens would seem to have actively participated in the conduct of government. However, by the end of the sixth century, thanks to Cleisthenes's reforms, a participatory democracy, at least in theory, had been created in Athens. Whether or not they did so, all citizens had the right to participate collectively in the government. The word *dēmos* referred to "the entire citizenry" and not just "the nonaristocracy." These *dēmoi* possessed *kratos*, or ruling power, hence, the word *democracy*.

As the century drew to a close, a new danger threatened the young Athenian democracy from outside. The Persians were looking west to Asia Minor for the further expansion of their immense empire. Under Cambyses, the Ionian cities on the coast of Asia Minor had already been deprived of their independence. Persian rule now extended from the Indus to the Aegean Sea. It was almost certain that the Persians would try to subdue the small Greek city-states on the frontier of their empire.

A woman gives a warrior a drink. Picture on the bottom of a *kylix* (drinking cup) from the fifth century BC

The Persian Wars

Greece's Perennial Conflict with Persia

Greek cities in Asia Minor were conquered by Croesus, the king of Lydia, and his predecessors during the course of the mid-sixth century BC and incorporated into the Lydian kingdom, to its general cultural, economic, and political benefit. Homer knew Lydia as Maeonia, the rising kingdom in the valleys of the Hermus and Cayster Rivers (now called the Gediz and Menderes, respectively). Under the Mermnadae, it had begun to gain

511

imperial importance about 685 BC, its economy fueled by its rich soil, its thriving industry and commerce, and its gold and silver.

The First Coins

Lydians minted (made) the first modern coins from these metals about 600 BC. They were fat disks stamped with pictures and their specified worth. Before this Lydian invention, most trade had been carried on by the direct exchange of merchandise. In some areas, grains of gold and silver or bars of gold, silver, or bronze were used to represent the value of goods. (The word *money* came later, taken from the Latin *moneta* or mint, an appellation for the Roman goddess Juno. Coins were made at her temple in Rome.)

Sardis

Under Croesus, who reigned from 560 to 546 BC, Lydia achieved its peak. The term *as rich as Croesus* refers to him. As he expanded the empire, he got richer on the booty he took. Croesus invested much of that wealth in his capital, Sardis. It lay near Mount Tmolus (now Boz Dag) on the Pactolus River (now the Baguli). (It would be conquered successively by the Persians, Macedonians, the Seleucids, the Romans, and the Mongols, who, under Tamerlane, destroyed it in 1402. It is mentioned in the Bible (Revelation 3:1) as one of the seven Christian churches of Asia. The ancient city was uncovered in AD 1958, although archaeological work had begun in its vicinity in 1910.

There is a story that when Athens's great legal reformer and philosopher Solon visited him, Croesus claimed to be the happiest man on earth because of his wealth. Solon reputedly (and prophetically) said: "Call no man happy before his death." Croesus was defeated and captured by Cyrus the Great around 546 BC.

Croesus, the king of Lydia, on the pyre. According to some, he was so threatened by his enemies that he wished to commit suicide in this way. Herodotus, however, states that he was sentenced to the pyre by Cyrus. Attic red-figured amphora from the fifth century BC

A *hoplite* (heavily armed soldier) has fallen in battle. Statue from the eastern pediment of the temple of Athena Aphaia on the island of Aegina, dating from between 490 and 480 BC

The Rise of Persia

Persia's rapid ascent to power in the sixth century BC was due to the efforts of Cyrus the Great, who reigned from 559 to 544 BC. Before he took the throne, the Persians were only one of the many small peoples in an Asia Minor dominated by Mesopotamia and Egypt. The new king consolidated his power at home and set out on foreign conquests. In 546 BC, he conquered Sardis, defeating the Lydians, the dominant power in the region. He made all of Greece except Samos and the islands part of his Persian Empire and used Sardis as its western capital. In 539 BC, his army seized Babylon, freeing the Jews from Babylonian captivity. The Persians stretched from the Aegean Sea to the Indus and from the Danube to the Red Sea, making Persia the largest kingdom up to that point in time.

Darius I, who reigned from 521 to 486 BC, wanted to round off the borders of the kingdom in India, far to the east of the Caspian Sea, in Armenia, in North Africa, and in the Aegean region. This Persian appetite for expansion led to a perennial con-

Bust of the Greek historian Herodotus (ca. 485–ca. 425 BC)

Attic red-figured vase
from the second half of the
fifth century BC.
Apollo and Artemis (her arm
is only just visible on
the left) kill Niobe's children
with arrows.

Bust of Themistocles,
Athenian statesman of the
early fifth century BC

flict between the Greeks and the Persians. By
512 BC, Darius had crossed the Bosporus
and was actively seeking conquests on the
west side of the Black Sea all the way to the
mouth of the Danube, with little success.

The regions where Greek poleis were situated, or where Greek was spoken in 500 BC,
were spread throughout the entire Greek
peninsula, the islands of the eastern
Mediterranean Sea, the coast of Asia Minor,
and the colonized areas around the Black
Sea, in Cyrene, on Sicily and in southern
Italy, the southern coast of France, and the
east coast of Spain. These areas did not constitute a political unit; the total area was
divided into hundreds of independent states
and mini-states. The Greeks of Asia Minor,
the Black Sea, and Cyrene were, in any case,
nominally under Persian sovereign authority,
since these regions were conquered in the

second half of the sixth century by Cyrus, Cambyses, and Darius. It was in these areas that the first open conflicts broke out.

Athens and Sparta had become the predominant city-states of Greece between the eighth and sixth centuries BC, following similar patterns of development and political strategy. Both had created confederacies under their control out of their weaker neighbors. Sparta was far more militaristic, establishing and maintaining its authority by the sword. The polis of Athens was formed by mutual agreement of the smaller cities of Attica. (Both the principal city and the larger city-state which comprised the surrounding region of Attica were called Athens.) Athenian citizenship was granted to freemen in all the outlying areas. Hereditary kingship had been ended by the *eupatridae* (nobles) in 683 BC. Draco, a notable statesman, codified Athenian law, defining the limits of the judiciary power of the nobles. Solon reformed the Draconian code in 594 BC.

The balance of power between Greece, led by Sparta and Athens, and Persia was the major subject of the historian Herodotus.

Herodotus

The most important source on the history of this period is the historian Herodotus from Halicarnassus in Asia Minor, born between the Persian Wars. Called the father of historiography by Cicero, he attempted to interpret the past, to put a human face and a moral understanding to it. According to Herodotus's own words, his work is the fruit of research and inquiry. Thus, he opens his work: "Here follows an explanation of the study that Herodotus of Halicarnassus initiated with the intention that the deeds of the people not be forgotten in time and that the important and amazing feats of the Greeks and non-Greeks be given their due glory, and also to shed light on the reason why they entered into conflict with one another."

The study to which he refers was based on his own travels throughout Asia Minor, Egypt, Palestine, Phoenicia, Mesopotamia, and the Black Sea region, and his more settled life in Athens and Thurii, an Athenian colony in southern Italy. His goal was to collect information, separating what he had seen and heard from other observations. His intellectual curiosity links him with the Ionian or pre-Socratic philosophers.

The Ionian Rebellion

In 499 BC, a massive rebellion against Persian dominance in Asia Minor broke out in the Ionian coastal cities and on the islands. The rebellion, at first successful, seems to have been inspired by economic motives.

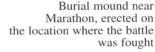

Burial mound near Marathon, erected on the location where the battle was fought

Bust of Cimon (fifth century BC) wearing a polemarch's helmet (a polemarch is a military commander in chief)

515

The Athenians' treasure house in Delphi, erected to thank Apollo for their victory at Marathon. It dates from around 490 BC and was built from part of the loot they gained at the battle.

The Persians had formed a formidable navy which threatened to damage the trading position of the Greek cities. The rebels turned to the continental Greeks for support. Only Athens, an Ionian city itself, closely tied with the sister cities of Asia Minor, and Eretria on Évvoia responded. Eretria sent squadrons of warships. Herodotus emphasizes the fact that the help from Eretria and Athens to the Ionians led to the Persian Wars. The Ionian cities, taking a democratic turn, drove out their ruling tyrants, who had functioned as figureheads for the Persians. The rebels went on to Sardis, where Artaphernes, brother of Darius, ruled as a *satrap* (despot). The Greeks succeeded in occupying the lower town by surprise, but did not take control of the citadel of Sardis. For lack of leadership, their retreat deteriorated into chaos. Artaphernes managed to catch up to them before they could reach the coast and inflicted a heavy defeat on the Greeks near Ephesus. The rebellion collapsed. In 495 BC, the Greeks lost an important sea battle by the coast of Asia Minor. In 493 BC, Darius I quashed the rebellion, demolishing Miletus, the largest city of Asia Minor and the center of the Greek rebellion, and deporting the residents to Mesopotamia. The other cities were punished according to their part in the rebellion. Darius reestablished control over Ionia.

The First Persian War

The next year, 492 BC, his son-in-law Mardonius led an unsuccessful attempt to annex Thrace and Macedonia, areas already influenced by the Persians but which had benefited from the Ionian rebellion. Mardonius's fleet was shipwrecked near Mount Athos on the Chalcidice peninsula.

Darius had learned enough from this rebellion over the years to make some concessions to the Greeks of Asia Minor and had relaxed his regime somewhat, not requiring the cities to take their old tyrants back. However, in 491, he sent heralds to the Greek poleis to send "earth and water" to him as a sign of submission. All the communities on the islands and various communities on the continent complied with this request, but Athens and Sparta not only refused, they killed the messengers.

Darius, outraged by that action and humiliated by the loss of his fleet, was readily deluded by two Greek exiles in his court who convinced him that they had a number of sympathizers in Greece. These two exiles were Hippias, the ex-tyrant of Athens, and Demaratus, an ex-king of Sparta. In 490 BC, Darius sent a second expedition to Greece, this time explicitly directed against Athens.

The captains were Datis and Artaphernes, cousin of Darius and son of the satrap Artaphernes. On board the Persian fleet was Hippias, convinced that he could regain his position of power with Persian support. The fleet sailed from the island of Samos, crossed the Aegean Sea, and destroyed Eretria, de-

porting its residents to the interior of Persia.

The Persian army, 20,000 to 25,000 strong, then went ashore from the Bay of Marathon, some twenty-five miles (40 kilometers) east of Athens. The Persians wanted to make contact with Hippias's sympathizers, who had his home base on that side of Attica. The Athenians sought assistance from Sparta but their request came during a religious festival which the Spartans would not leave. As soon as the Athenians learned of the landing near Mara-

Monument in commemoration of the battle of Marathon (490 BC). It is a modern copy of a classical grave relief.

517

Helmet of Miltiades,
commander of the Athenians
at Marathon.
His name is inscribed
on the edge.

thon, however, they sent 10,000 Athenian hoplites and a contingent of 1,000 Plataean soldiers. The Athenian general Miltiades argued for an attack, but the Athenians were outnumbered three to one and had no cavalry. After a few days of waiting on both sides, the Athenians noticed that the Persians had embarked, probably to sail around Attica and try from the other side. When the Persian cavalry was on board, the Athenians attacked, defeating the Persians. According to Herodotus, 6,400 Persians and 192 Greeks died at Marathon. The first figure may be exaggerated, but the accuracy of the second has been confirmed by excavation of the burial mound of the Athenian soldiers. From AD 1969 to 1970, a second burial mound was examined, suspected to be that of the Plataean soldiers.

The Marathon

The Athenians sent a Greek runner to take the news the twenty-five miles (forty kilometers) to Athens. When the Olympic Games were revived in 1896 in Athens, they included a long-distance foot race at about that distance. It was called the marathon in honor of this 490 BC event. (Marathon race distance has now been standardized at 26 miles, 385 yards (42.2 kilometers).

Attack on Athens

After the unexpected defeat at Marathon, the Persian fleet sailed around Cape Sunion to undertake a second landing attempt and march on the now-unprotected Athens. The army of Athenian civilians, however, returned to the city in a forced march within seven hours. To add to this, the Persians must have learned that the Spartan army was rapidly advancing toward Athens. Discouraged, the Persian fleet retreated. The great victory for the Athenians was, for the Persians, only a skirmish without much significance and certainly no reason to give up their attention to Greece.

The Second Persian War

The next Persian attack came ten years later. The delay was caused by Darius's death in 486 BC and the subsequent domestic disturbances which forced his son Xerxes I, to wait until 481 BC. According to Herodotus, Xerxes was warned against the consequences of a new adventure by the highest advisory bodies, but the king continued his preparations for what would become the largest military undertaking in history.

Athens had made good use of the ten-year calm. The city had transformed itself into a naval power. The events of the Ionian rebellion had demonstrated the importance of a strong fleet. Miltiades, the victor at Marathon, had made a start in this direction at Marathon and had begun to undermine Persian power in the Aegean Sea when he was fatally wounded during the unsuccessful siege of the island of Paros. His role was taken over by Themistocles, who, as *archon* (chief magistrate), had started expanding Piraeus into the new harbor of Athens. Themistocles had seen a number of his opponents banished over the years. By 483 BC, he seemed to be the only person of any importance in Athenian politics. He convinced the Athenians to spend the major part of the profits gained from the newly opened silver mines of Laurium on shipbuilding. The army was neglected to favor superiority on the sea. The number of Athenian warships rose from seventy to two hundred.

In 481 BC, when the Persian preparations for the new war were already under way, a conference of Greek states met in Corinth, probably at Themistocles's instigation, to confer on the tactics to be followed. It was decided to proclaim an overall peace to end the ongoing internal conflict. (Both Sparta and Athens were at war with neighboring states.) All exiles, including the ostracized Athenians, were to be called back. All states would enter into an alliance against Persia, with no consideration of any separate peace. The property of traitors would be expropriated and given to the sanctuary in Delphi.

Despite this friendly gesture toward the oracle, its prophecies there were unfavorable. Apparently the people in Delphi were so well informed of the Persians' formidable war preparations that they dared recommend no less than unconditional surrender. The advice of the oracle "to flee to the ends of the earth" was not at all appreciated by the Athenians. They asked the oracle for a less defeatist counsel. It responded that only "wooden walls" could protect Athens. That means ships, declared Themistocles in the assembly. This was a wise idea, regardless of the oracle, since the ships were essentially ready. Thirty other Greek states had decided to join with Athens in meeting the Persian attack head-on. Sparta was put in charge of the entire military.

On the Persian side, Xerxes I was personally in charge of the new expedition. The winter of 481-480 BC was devoted to preparations in Sardis. Measures were also taken all along the marching route into northern

Bust of Miltiades, commander of the Athenians at Marathon

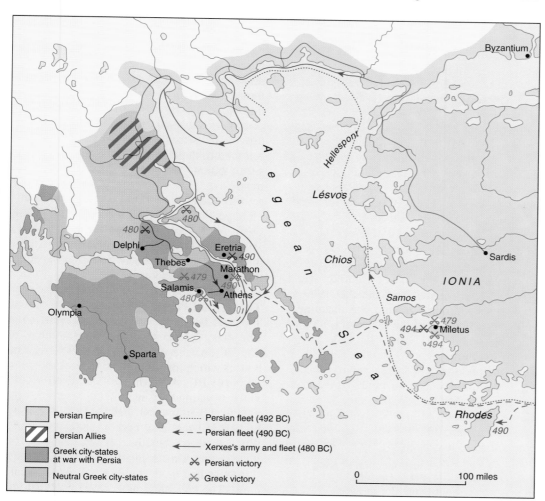

▢ Persian Empire	⋯◀⋯ Persian fleet (492 BC)
▨ Persian Allies	— ◀ — Persian fleet (490 BC)
▨ Greek city-states at war with Persia	◀——— Xerxes's army and fleet (480 BC)
▢ Neutral Greek city-states	✕ Persian victory
	✕ Greek victory

0   100 miles

Map depicting the course of the Persian Wars

519

Modern view of Plataea, the region where the Spartans beat the Persians (479 BC)

Detail of the monument erected near Thermopylae in commemoration of King Leonidas and the Spartans

Greece. The Persian army was one of the largest that had ever been assembled. It was too large to be transported by sea and too large to live off the land it had to pass through. Food transport by sea was essential. Xerxes was forced to follow the old road via the Bosporus. In 480 BC, he led the Persians over a bridge of boats across the Hellespont strait and trekked into Europe within a few days.

The army followed the coastal route south. A large fleet of warships and freight vessels went down along the coast at the same time. They were ordered not to lose sight of each other, because the Persian land army could not function without the fleet.

From Thessaly to central Greece, the road runs through the pass of Thermopylae between the sea and the mountains. (The present site bears little resemblance to the original, due to alluvial deposits.) The Greek army waited at the pass for the Persians. A route any farther inland would have been unsuitable for the Persians who had to stay in contact with the fleet. An army of 9,000 heavily armed soldiers, including three hundred Spartans, made camp in the pass under command of the Spartan king Leonidas.

The Greeks could have easily defeated the

Persians but for the treason of a Greek guide. He showed the Persians a mountain pass, allowing them to get behind the Greek lines. The danger was seen in time to avoid the massacre of the full Greek army. The Spartan leader Leonidas, 1,300 Spartans, and 700 Thespians were slaughtered covering the retreat of several thousand soldiers.

Central Greece and Attica lay open to the advancing enemy. On Themistocles's advice, the population of Athens was evacuated to Salamis and the Peloponnisos. A wise decision, because Xerxes had Athens absolutely demolished. Themistocles had to watch the clouds of smoke rise from the burning temples on the Acropolis from Salamis, an island in the Gulf of Aegina near Athens.

The Greek fleet escaped after three undecided naval battles that caused extensive damage to the Persian ships. The Persians pursued the Greek fleet to Salamis. According to the poet Aeschylus, who took part in the ensuing battle, the Persian fleet chose a position blocking eastern access to the Bay of Elensis. This fleet made such an impression that the Spartan leaders proposed retreating from the bay via the western

access, with the intent of assembling all land and naval forces by the isthmus of Corinth and building a wall to block the Persians. Themistocles convinced his allies not to flee: what was the use of a wall if the Persian fleet could sail past it? Only "wooden walls" could help.

The Persians were sure of impending victory. Xerxes had a golden throne built on a hill overlooking the harbor of Salamis to witness the anticipated destruction of the Greek fleet. At this decisive point, Themistocles sent a messenger to Xerxes with false information on dissension among the Greeks. The Athenians, he was told, wanted to defect to the enemy. The Persians had to attack right away if they wanted to take advantage of the situation. The ruse worked. The Persian fleet sailed to Salamis expecting to destroy the Greek fleet in the bay. Three hundred Greek ships were pitted against roughly 350 Persian ships: the rest had been directed to the other end of the bay or had been knocked out of action earlier. The naval battle broke out at daybreak. In the narrow bay, less than a mile (1.6 kilometers) wide, the maneuverable Greek ships had the advantage. The

Detail of an Athenian vase depicting farmers harvesting olives

Attic red-figured
plate, decorated by Epiketos
around 520 BC
with a picture of a Scythian
archer

wind was in their favor, as well, and a few Ionian ships had joined them, turning against the largely Phoenician and Egyptian squadrons which formed the Persian fleet. The Greeks, appearing to retreat, lured the Persian ships deeper in the bay and then attacked. By evening, Xerxes could see his fleet was crushed. Fewer than 400 Greek ships had defeated 1,200 Persian vessels.

Xerxes retreated to Asia with a large part of the army but left a strong contingent to spend the winter in central Greece and Macedonia. This army was under the command of Mardonius who had led the expedition in 492 BC. This general rightly assumed that if he retreated north, the Spartans would leave their position on the isthmus and return home. His plan was to negotiate a settlement with the Athenians without Sparta. At the start of the new war season in the spring of 479 BC, Mardonius sent a delegation to Athens offering to repair all damage and help in reconstructing the city. He asked Athens to recognize the sovereignty of the Persian king in exchange.

The Athenians did not agree to Mardonius's proposals and reassured the concerned Spartans that they would stand firm for "the Greek brotherhood, the collective ancestry and language, and the altars and the sacrifices in which all Greeks share," as Herodotus put it.

Mardonius responded by ravaging Attica, but he pulled back his troops when the Spartan main force advanced to the north. Sparta sent its entire army, supplemented by civilian *perioikoi* (free indigenous people from the outskirts of Sparta) and even *helots* (indigenous serfs), a total of 45,000 men. Athens contributed another 8,000 *hoplites* (foot soldiers). Never before had such a massive army assembled in Greece. Pausanias, regent for the under-age Spartan king, was in command. After three weeks of waiting at Plataea, Pausanias had had to move his troops because the Persian cavalry had taken possession of his water sources. A Spartan unit refused to retreat with him. Mardonius thought he could take advantage of the confusion, but in the chaotic battle that ensued, the Greeks emerged victors. When they overpowered the enemy camp and killed Mardonius, the battle was decided. Meanwhile, at Cape Mycale near Miletus in Ionia, the Persian fleet suffered a fatal blow. The Persian forces in the Aegean Sea were overwhelmed. The Greek city-states, led by Athens and Sparta, defeated the mighty empire of the Persians.

Illyrian helmet
from the time of the
Persian Wars

Part of the grand cavalry procession on the occasion of the Panathenaea festival in Athens, on the north frieze of the cella on the Parthenon (ca. 440 BC)

The Age of Pericles

The Flowering of Athenian Democracy

Pericles (ca. 495-429 BC)

The Athenian statesman Pericles was so important to the development of Athens that historians give his name to the time he was in power in the fifth century BC. He would overshadow his father Xanthippus, who avenged the 480 BC burning of Athens by defeating the Persians at Mycale in 479 BC. As leader of the popular party and head of state (after 460 BC), Pericles led Athens to its greatest splendor.

The Rise of Athens

Themistocles's brilliant victory off the island of Salamis in the Gulf of Aegina marked the rise of Athenian sea power. (With less than 400 Greek crafts, he defeated 1,200 Persian ships.)With the final Persian defeat at Plataea in 479 BC, Athens became the predominant city-state in Greece.

Sparta, which had been the greatest military power in Greece, now lost place to Athens and opted for temporary isolation. The Persian slaughter at the mountain pass of Thermopylae the previous year had served to enhance the state's reputation for bravery. The Spartan Leonidas I and 1,400 soldiers, 300 of them Spartan, had been killed, their

523

A so-called Athenian owl
(5th century BC).
These coins were struck
in Athens; the owl symbolizes
the goddess Athena.

vanguard position revealed to the Persians by the Thessalian Ephialtes. Their deaths allowed the main Greek army to retreat.

The Spartans returned to their austere life on the Peloponnisos Peninsula, their lands untouched by the Persian Wars. Since the sixth century, they had organized their society as a disciplined military force, compelling service beginning with drill for all boys at the age of seven. Although they had ample ability and resources to establish military sovereignty throughout Greece, for a time they concentrated on domestic affairs. A *helot* (slave) rebellion of serious proportion broke out in 464 BC.

Athens had suffered heavily from the war and it remained fearful of a new invasion. The Athenians supported offensive action to further weaken the Persians and reduce the threat. They had a powerful fleet, and, after Salamis and Mykale, undisputed supremacy in the eastern Mediterranean. Athens adopted a new and expensive expansion policy. Maintaining a fleet of sufficient size exceeded the funds of little Attica, the region surrounding the city. Athens had a vested interest in continuing joint efforts against Persia.

The Delian League

In 477 BC, Athens and most of the Aegean city-states formed an alliance against Persia called the Delian League (also the Sea Alliance or Confederation of Delos). It was named for the island of Delos, where the meetings were to take place and alliance funds were to be kept. Athens headed the league, but all members, in principle, had equal vote. Athens commanded a fleet of two hundred ships, asking every ally to pay an annual fee to maintain it. Contributions of ships, men, and equipment were required, proportionate to resources.

Under the joint command of Generals Cimon and Aristides, the Greeks freed the coasts of the Aegean from Persian control between 476 and 466 BC. Cimon alone led the destruction of both a Persian fleet of two hundred ships near the Eurymedon River (Turkey) and Persian land forces on the same day in 466 BC.

By this time, most allies were paying Athens their assessed contributions in money

The Charioteer
of Delphi, a bronze statue
that was donated to the
temple of Apollo in Delphi
as a votive gift,
ca. 470 BC

rather than material, tantamount to tribute. When Naxos objected, attempting to withdraw from the league, Athens destroyed its forts. It annexed the land of other recalcitrant allies, distributing it to the Athenians. The goal had been preparation against Persian aggression. The result was a naval empire run by Athens that encompassed, as equals or subjected allies, most of the large islands of the Aegean Sea and many cities to the north.

In 464 BC, Cimon sided with Athens's arch rival Sparta against rebelling helots. He was ostracized in Athens and banished from the city in 461 BC. Pericles was made head of state in 460 BC, serving the next fifteen years. About 444 BC, he brought the league treasury from Delos to Athens, financing expensive building projects in Athens.

The battle with Persia ended with the Peace of Callias in 449 BC. With the Persian threat gone and Athens in control, neighboring city-states on the Greek mainland joined the league. The allies of the Delian League had become vassals of Athens.

The Peloponnesian War (431-404 BC)
The city-state of Corinth grew concerned with the success of Athens's imperialism under Pericles. Developing from an ancient settlement near the isthmus of Corinth, it had become a thriving trade city under the

Picture of a *symposium* (drinking feast) with a performance by a flute player. Decoration of an Attic cup, ca. 460 BC

Bust of Pericles (copy from an original, ca. 425 BC). Pericles was the leader of Athens between 460 and 429 BC. He was an extraordinarily able general; during his rule, Athenian expansion and prosperity surpassed everything that had preceded it.

525

The Acropolis of Athens. The large building in the middle is the Parthenon.

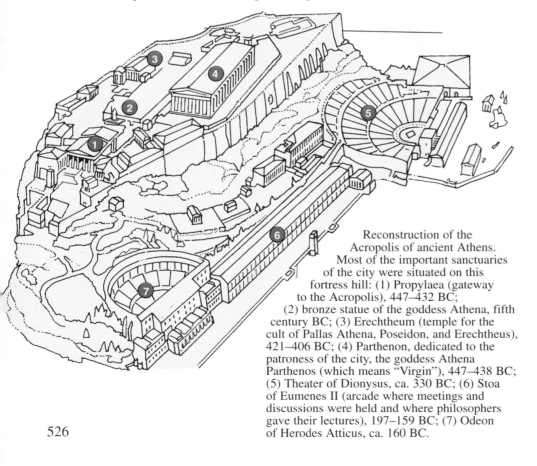

Reconstruction of the Acropolis of ancient Athens. Most of the important sanctuaries of the city were situated on this fortress hill: (1) Propylaea (gateway to the Acropolis), 447–432 BC; (2) bronze statue of the goddess Athena, fifth century BC; (3) Erechtheum (temple for the cult of Pallas Athena, Poseidon, and Erechtheus), 421–406 BC; (4) Parthenon, dedicated to the patroness of the city, the goddess Athena Parthenos (which means "Virgin"), 447–438 BC; (5) Theater of Dionysus, ca. 330 BC; (6) Stoa of Eumenes II (arcade where meetings and discussions were held and where philosophers gave their lectures), 197–159 BC; (7) Odeon of Herodes Atticus, ca. 160 BC.

Dorians by 1000 BC. Benefiting from its harbors on the Corinthian and Saronic gulfs, by 650 BC, it was the major center of commerce in Greece. Corinth established many colonies, notably Corcyra and Syracuse in the eighth century BC and Potidaea in the seventh century BC. As Athens increased its naval and commercial activity, the older trade city felt particularly threatened.

In 431 BC, Corinth joined Sparta in forming the Spartan Confederacy to counteract the rising power of the Delian League. Thebes, Macedonia, and Ambracia on the Ionian seacoast allied with them. They faced Athens's power all along the northern and eastern coasts of the Aegean, on most of the large islands in that sea, and in Byzantium. The rivalry between Sparta and Athens had erupted into the Peloponnesian War.

Pericles called all the country residents of Attica, the region surrounding Athens, inside the city walls for safety. The army of the Spartan Confederacy pillaged unimpeded through the rural area. The next year (430 BC), plague decimated overcrowded Athens. Pericles was deposed from office by his angry and dying people. He was tried and fined for misuse of public funds. Briefly

reinstated, he died in 429 BC. Athens, defeated as much by disease and unfortunate expansion policies, surrendered to Sparta in 404 BC.

Democracy in Athens

The period of Athenian domination under Pericles is called the Golden Age, and it can be said of its government as well as its culture. The constitution was modified to further internal democracy, and the power of the aristocracy continued to break down. In 487 BC, it was decided that the highest magistrates, the archons, would be drawn by lot, rather than elected. The magistracy consequently lost importance, as did the Areopagus, the old council of nobility to which ex-archons belonged. In 462 BC, the judicial function of the Areopagus was largely taken over by jury tribunals, and its supervision over all administrators of the polis was relegated to the Council of 500.

Around the middle of the century, the archontate was opened to citizens of the third-highest class of society. A policy of payment of attendance fees to magistrates, council members, and jury members was adopted. At the beginning of the fourth century BC, this payment was extended to fees for attendance at public meetings. This allowed the exercise of political rights without the worry of financial stress. It was of particular benefit to the *thetes*, empowering them to take part in the government of the polis. It reflected their importance as rowers of the Athenian fleet.

The Political Leaders

The selection of magistrates by lot carried some risks. Some aspects of government required a degree of specialized knowledge not available to the common man. In an effort to deal with this, the Athenians created the ten elected positions of *stratēgos*, who were appointed for only one year. They could be reelected, but were subject to mon-

The Parthenon on the Acropolis of Athens. The Persians sacked Athens, including the Acropolis, in 480 BC; Pericles began construction of the Parthenon in 447 BC, using funds of the Delian League.

527

Servants with sacrificial animals, walking in the grand procession depicted on the cella frieze of the Parthenon (ca. 440 BC)

itoring and evaluation by their nine fellow *stratēgos.* They could be removed from office by the public meeting. As is evident, there was little chance of a *stratēgos* becoming a tyrant.

Given the size of the assembly, only a few of those present could have time to speak. The issues were often complicated and not everyone could be expected to speak with equal authority. Addressing several thousand people (and convincing them to vote the way the speaker wanted) was not possible for everyone. A new class of orator-politicians, called *rhetors,* developed in the fifth century. They played a leading role in political decision making. Pericles is the most famous of them and certainly the most important.

Rhetors spoke on their own behalf or on behalf of ad hoc interest groups. They were not politicians representing political parties; these did not exist in the modern sense. Athenian democracy, in theory, allowed participation in political life by nonelite and elite, but it was not until the second half of the fifth century that nonaristocrats (generally wealthy and sophisticated) were called on as designated speakers in the public assembly.

An expansive democratic spirit predominated in Athens. A famous funeral oration illustrates it, spoken to honor those killed in the first year (AD 431) of the Peloponnesian War. The historian Thucydides, attributed it to his contemporary Pericles. The text

Women in Classical Athens

The land of powerful goddesses and female oracles was still a very young civilization, so Greek men viewed Greek women largely in terms of their bodies. Women were categorized into four groups by their ability to bear children: the young, sexually immature girl; the marriageable virgin; the sexually active, fertile wife and mother; and the elderly, infertile. Outside of this classification, and essentially outside of society, fell marriageable women who had lost their virginity and infertile women, including prostitutes. This infertility was usually not biological in origin, unless caused by disease, but artificial; both contraception and abortion were practiced by the Greeks.

Women (and men) were expected to marry and to procreate. The married couple was considered an economic unit. Marriage was regarded primarily as a rational matter (although this did not exclude love or affection). Usually, the fathers of the bride and groom made a contractual agreement, although the father of the bride could also make an agreement with the future husband. The bride was typically much younger than her bridegroom. In classical Athens, she was about fourteen and he was in his late twenties. The wife adopted a subordinate position; Greek society was strictly patriarchal. The woman's place was in the house. Women, in theory, only left the house to attend funerals and religious celebrations, but there were, in fact, many religious events where women played an important role. Men were usually outside the home, leaving it at will for work, political life, or social reasons. Men and women of the middle and upper classes lived in distinctly separate spheres of life. This separation was less evident among the poor. They could not afford personnel and were forced to have their female relatives work with them.

Most Greek men were convinced of the inferiority of women, both physically and mentally. While this was not true in terms of women's potential, it was, in some sense, an accurate description of their condition. Women did not eat as well as men, got little exercise, and suffered the complications of pregnancy and a variety of female ailments. They were generally given no opportunity for education. The fact that women were seen as inferior meant that they were always treated as minors. They were not permitted to act independently. Women always had to be represented by an adult male, called the *kurios* (guardian). Thus, a woman was successively under the *kurieia* (guardianship) of her father, husband, adult son, or some other male relative.

Attic red-figured amphora, ca. 440 BC, with a picture of women making music illustrates Athenian ideology:

"Our government is no imitation of our neighbors. To the contrary: we are an example for them. We are a democracy, because the government is in the hands of the people and not in the hands of a small group; but our law explicitly states that every citizen has equal rights. We Athenians recognize the supremacy of intelligence, and when a fellow citizen clearly distinguishes himself from the others, the people appoint him to the highest positions. This is not the right of a gifted man, but the reward for his great merits. Lack of money is no obstacle in fulfilling high offices: any citizen can serve the fatherland. There are no privileges in our political life, nor in our personal relationships; we trust one another. While we give each other freedom in our private lives, we show mutual understanding with respect to our public deeds. The respect for legal authority and state law prevents us from acting wrongfully. We have great appreciation for those who are chosen to protect the weak, and our moral law punishes the offenders with a unanimous feeling of condemnation.

"Neither do we Athenians forget the importance of relaxation for our tired minds. We have feasts and ceremonies throughout the year. Life is pleasant in our homes, and with our noble behavior, we provide ourselves with pleasures which hinder sadness. The fame of our city brings us fruits from the entire Earth, so that we can enjoy foreign and exotic products. Our military organization is better than that of our adversaries. Moreover, our city is open to everyone; we have never driven out foreigners. We do everything in public and are not afraid that our deeds will reach the enemy. For our defense we do not rely on complicated organizations, nor on unworthy means, but on the courage of the heart and the strength of our arms. We are admirers of beauty, but we remain simple.

Attic red-figured *hydria* (water jar, ca. 430 BC), found in a grave on the Athens grave field of Kerameikos

The Strangford Shield, a small copy made in the third century AD of the shield that belonged with the statue of Athena Parthenon in the Parthenon. In the middle of the shield, a gorgon's head can be seen; around it, an *Amazonomachia* (a fight between Amazons and Greeks) is going on.

We do not flaunt our wealth; we use it where it is needed. For us, honest poverty is no disgrace. A citizen of Athens does not shirk back from state affairs in order to pursue exclusively his own activities. Also those of us who are involved in big business stay abreast of government matters. Anyone who does not wish to be involved with public affairs we do not consider indifferent, but dangerous! And although there are few among us who are extraordinary enough to formulate proposals, we are all good enough to make decisions. It is our conviction that danger does not lie in discussion, but in ignorance. We have the special characteristic that we can think before we act, and even in the middle of action. Others, on the other hand, are brave in ignorance, yet hesitate as soon as they begin to think!"

Here Athens is praising Athens, for its power, strength, prosperity, openness, freedom, equality of the citizens, and so on. In the parts not quoted, the text shifts to the glorious history of Athens, the great Athenian Empire, and the courage of Athenian fighters. It is an idealization of Athenian democracy and the Athenian citizen. There is no reference to slavery; a definite aspect of Athenian society, it was accepted as a matter of course by most Greeks, including Pericles.

Anti-Democrats
A political pamphlet by an anonymous author from this era summarizes a number of objections to democracy that were prevalent in Athens. Although the pamphleteer wrote in rebuttal to these opinions, he offers a good impression of the ideological views opposing those expressed in Pericles's oration.

Arguing against open and equal participation in government, he writes: "One can argue that not every Tom, Dick, or Harry should be allowed to speak and sit on the

Part of the Erechtheum, with the famous karyatids, columns in the shape of women carrying the roof of the building on their heads, on the right

531

The Varvakeion Athena (made in the second or third century AD), a small copy of the much taller statue of Athena Parthenon that was made by the sculptor Pheidias (447–438 BC). His statue, which he made for the Parthenon, measured forty feet (twelve meters), and was decorated with gold and ivory.

council, but only the best and most intelligent citizens...how can such a low person decide what is good for himself or for the entire *dēmos* (populace)?" The principal motive of the critics of democracy was that "good government" was impossible when it was left to "madmen."

Plato, certainly no supporter of democracy, had similar views. In the *Republic,* he called democracy anarchy, contending that the people only listen to themselves: "... with a sort of equality not only for the equals, but also for the unequals."

He also wrote, "Whenever a meeting must be held concerning matters of state, the one to stand up and offer advice can be a carpenter, a smith, a shoemaker, a merchant, a shipowner, a rich man, a poor man, of good family, or of no family at all, and no one thinks of telling him that his meddling is not justified by any knowledge of matters, nor by the instruction of a teacher."

Such opinions were held by Athenians inclined toward *oligarchy* (government by the few) certainly present in democratic Athens, even if they played no major political role. They were admirers of Sparta, a state where, it was said, at least everyone knew his place.

Only in the final quarter of the fifth century BC, when Athens was at war with Sparta (which ended in Athens's defeat), did the oligarchs have the opportunity to attempt to change the radical Athenian democracy. Their efforts did not last long and had no lasting impact.

Culture

Thanks to the Sea Alliance, Athens was both powerful and prosperous, with the considerable earnings of the silver mines of Attica and the harbor dues of Piraeus, the most important port on the eastern Mediterranean.

Athens was an open society, powerful and wealthy, interested in intellectual pursuits in every area of human endeavor. Its Golden Age witnessed an explosion of creative culture. Athens developed into an important center of philosophy and science, for the first time. Philosophers came from all corners of the world and found welcome amid the well-to-do. Philosophy became the fashion, its

Athenian jar (ca. 500 BC) with a picture of four runners in a race

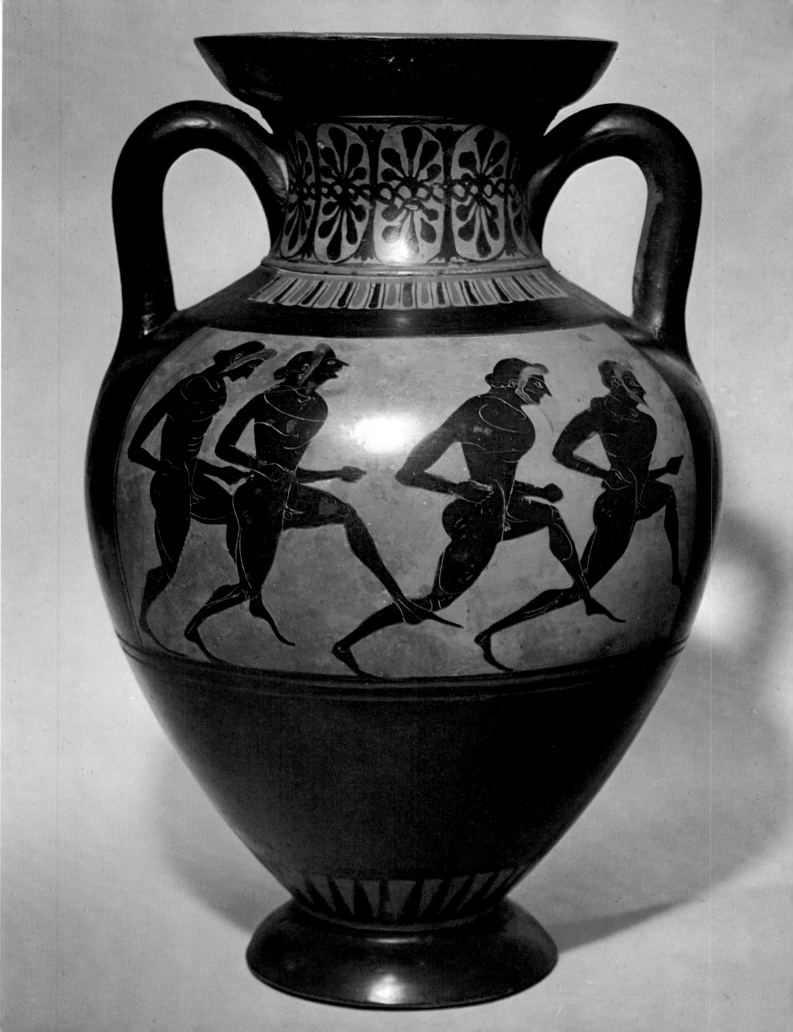

leaders were Anaxagoras, Socrates, Plato, Herodotus, and Thucydides.

Pericles himself was especially influenced by two teachers, the Athenian Sophist and master of music Damon (of the fifth century BC) and the Ionian philosopher Anaxagoras. Throughout his life he was noted for his aloofness, but his eloquence, wisdom, and patriotism won recognition from the majority of citizens. Among his friends were the playwright Sophocles, the historian Herodotus, the sculptor Phidias, and the Sophist Protagoras. His mistress was the former courtesan Aspasia, a highly cultivated woman.

Pericles founded the colony of Thurii on the Gulf of Tarentum in southern Italy in 443 BC. He intended it to be a model colony with participants from all over Greece, the Aegean Islands, and Ionia. All sorts of famous figures became involved. The philosopher Protagoras of Abdera is said to have written its laws. The famous architect and urban developer Hippodamus of Miletus, designer of the city of Piraeus, supposedly did the colony's systematic city plan. Piraeus featured a street plan (called Hippodamian) of straight streets crossing each other to form rectangular blocks. Whether Thurii had such a plan has not yet been confirmed by archaeology.

The literary arts flourished in Athens. Greek tragedy was at its peak with the poetry and plays of Aeschylus, Sophocles, and Euripides. Euripides was reputed to have been born on the day of the battle of Salamis. Aeschylus fought in it. The great comedy writer Aristophanes was at work in this era, as well.

After the destruction of the Acropolis by the Persians in 480 BC, the Athenians had vowed never to build there again. They had left the ruins as a memorial to Persian barbarity. As they regained confidence and power over the fifth and fourth centuries BC, however, this viewpoint changed. Pericles restored the temples destroyed by the Persians and built many new structures. This program provided employment for the poorer citizens and made Athens the most magnificent city of the ancient world. The great Phidias sculpted a statue of the goddess Athena almost forty feet (approximately twelve meters) high for the Parthenon. This was one of the most admired pieces of art in ancient times. Unfortunately only copies and illustrations of them remain, but Phidias's workplace has been found in Olympia.

The great building projects of the fifth century attest to the blossoming of architecture. The buildings on the Acropolis, the Parthenon, the Propylaea, the little temple of Athena Nike, and the Erechtheum, all built of marble in the years from 447 to 406 BC, are extraordinary examples. The cultural growth of Athens was a result of both its economic and its political power.

Epilogue

The Delian League was reestablished in 377 BC by Greek city-states concerned about rising Spartan might. In 371 BC, under the leadership of Epaminondas, Thebes arranged a peace accord with Sparta that set it back inside its original borders. The once powerful state was forced to yield the territory it had conquered. The members of the Delian League were once more nominally subject to Athens, but Athens had no power of enforcement. The league finally ended in 338 BC, with the defeat of Athens by Philip II of Macedonia at Chaeronea.

Two *lebedes gamikoi*
(special vases, made for weddings; they are used with the bride's ritual bath). Attic red-figured earthenware, ca. 430 BC, found in a grave

Bust of Dionysus, the god of wine, drunkenness, and theater, made in the Hellenistic period. He was usually portrayed wearing a beard; however, in later art he emerges as a young man with a *thyrsus* (staff, wound with vine and ivy).

Greek Theater

A New Art Form Takes Shape

Dionysus

Theater in classical Athens was not worldly entertainment. It formed a part of the annual festivals honoring the god Dionysus. Dionysus was a very popular god, the god of wine, intoxication, and ecstasy. The word *ecstasy* implies more than simply intoxication. It can be interpreted to mean a way of losing yourself, of becoming one with the godhead, or of feeling at one with another person. Dionysus was also regarded as the god of reproduction and sexual drive, of the life force of all living beings. Ecstasy also implies a loss of self-control or insanity; hence, Dionysus was also viewed as the god of confusion, destruction, and death, all recognized as facets of human life. He was worshiped in all sorts of cults, including orgiastic. In some sense, Dionysus was considered the god of the whole of life, in all its aspects.

The inside of an Attic red-figured *kylix* (drinking cup) on which two satyrs dance around the god Dionysus. This picture was painted by the Brygos painter, ca. 500–480 BC.

If we now look at the theater, we see that only a few Greek dramas have plots directly connected with this god, yet it was said in Athens that if a play or a topic "had nothing to do with Dionysus," it made no sense at all. That's because it had nothing to do with life.

The Prehistory and Early History of the Drama

Much was written about the origins of Greek theater in ancient times, and modern scholars have produced entire libraries of commen-

tary. Regardless, we have no material on this subject. Even Aristotle, writing in the fourth century BC, noted few actual details on the roots of drama, preferring to present various hypotheses instead. There are many theories about the sources from which the drama could have been derived as it took shape in Athens during the sixth and fifth centuries. These include fertility rites, ancestral and heroic cults, ritual dances portrayed on archaic painted vases, and poetic recitation.

In the case of the tragedy, it is poetic

recitation that is most important, particularly in the Dionysian hymns called *dithyrambs.* These were choral lyrics sung in honor of Dionysus. The one who transformed dithyrambs is said to have been Arion from the island Lésvos. He worked in Corinth in the early sixth century under the tyrant Periander. Arion has also been credited with development of the tragic mode, later used extensively in Greek drama. In the tragic mode he concentrated on the more narrative material in the dithyrambs.

The singling out of an actor from the chorus reciting the dithyramb (or another piece of poetry) was the next step. Various sources mention the sixth-century BC chorus master and poet Thespis (probably a name chosen by the artist rather than his actual one and the source of a synonym for dramatic, thespian). They say that the statesman Solon was interested in the new works that Thespis had devised. He attended a performance, but after it was over, Solon was said to have reprimanded Thespis because he had so unabashedly "lied" to the public, by introducing a person who played a part to convince an audience.

Thespis had apparently introduced the role-playing actor to the new world of theater. If this was indeed a renewal created by Thepsis, it is enough to justify the description of Thespis as "the inventor of the tragedy." Thespis was a writer, a composer, a choreographer, a director, and an actor all in one. The name for such a chorus master actor was *tragoidos* (goat bard), probably because of the fact that tragoidoi took part in a competition that awarded a goat as the winning prize. *Tragoidia* (tragedy) was then supposedly derived from tragoidos.

The poet-dramatist Aeschylus later introduced a second actor, which laid the foundation for the development of what we call drama.

In Athens, under the tyrant Peisistratus, performances of tragedy and competitions among poets were the heart of the newly established Great Dionysian festival. Dithyrambs were omitted. Apparently their absence was considered disturbing, however, because Athens added them to the official festival around 500 BC. Dithyrambs were followed by a satyr play, usually with a heroic theme and a chorus of satyrs that lent a lighthearted tone to the production.

Festive processions, called *komoi*, were established, not as part of the competitions, but to make up the last element of the program, a comedy. Here, the *komos* (from which the word *komoidia* is derived) is the most important element. The komos was part of all sorts of Dionysian celebrations. It featured masquerades (such as animal guises) and singing competitions. Although all sorts of subjects were parodied, the comedies always had the very Dionysian atmosphere of rough merrymaking.

In the case of both the satyr plays and comedies, a Dionysian background is easily recognizable. While it was not usually incorporated in the theme, it was present in the performance. This was not the case with tragedy, even in its earliest form. This raises the question as to why tragedies were included in the festivals of Dionysus.

The answer may lie in thinking of Dionysus as the god of ecstasy, man "going

outside of himself." Acting itself involves going outside one's self to "become" another person. Seen this way, adopting a role is a very Dionysian activity. The elusive character of the god was symbolized by the mask, which played an important role in the cult of Dionysus. Masks were also worn in ancient theater, another link with the god.

Relief from the Hellenistic period on which Dionysus pays a visit to the Icarians. To thank them for their warm welcome, the god taught the Icarians how to grow grapes for wine production.

The Great Dionysia
Going to the theater was never simply a night out, but a ritual occasion. The Great Dionysia in Athens were held in the month Elaphebolion (March/April). Every year, a wooden stage and wooden bleachers were set up in the agora, usually the public square. Halfway through the fifth century, the stands collapsed. The accident resulted in the building of a new theater on the south slope of the Acropolis, near an existing shrine to Dionysus. (The remains of the theater visible today date from the fourth century BC and include later renovations.)

537

538

Terra-cotta
statue of an actor,
ca. fourth century BC

The theater of Dionysus in Athens (built ca. 500 BC, and several times reconstructed in later periods)

Mask for an actor, made in the Hellenistic period

The festivals lasted five days and nights. On the first day, there was a great procession and offerings were brought to Dionysus, followed by the dithyrambs competition, an impressive spectacle with ten boys' choruses and ten men's choruses of fifty singers each. That day closed with a komos procession. Four days of drama followed. On the first one, five comedies by five different authors were performed. Each of the next three days featured a tetralogy (three tragedies and a satyr play), contributed by a single author.

The eight authors chosen to challenge each other for the best comedy and tetralogy were selected by the *archons* (magistrates). These magistrates then looked for *choregi* (literal meaning is "chorus leader," closest to our concept of "producer"), wealthy people who were obliged to pay the costs of the event. The choregi searched for citizens who would pay for a spot in the chorus. Those who refused were fined. After a long period of rehearsals under the direction of the dramatist-poet, the performance was given. One dithyramb chorus was chosen by a jury as the winning company. One comedy and one tetralogy were selected as the winning pieces. The choregi of the winning choruses and pieces shared the honor. The jury was a committee of ten members who were chosen by lot (as was customary in democratic Athens).

The chorus dominated Greek theater in the fifth century; in a certain sense, the theater was derived from it. The chorus, with fifty members for the dithyrambs (twelve and later fifteen for the tragedy, and twenty-four for the comedy) recited or sang the text and emphasized the words with gestures or dance steps. For the Greeks, the dance figures were an essential part of the theater. The great care taken with the colorful costumes of the actors added greatly to the overall impression of the plays.

It is not entirely clear whether the actors spoke from a sort of platform or whether they also took their places on the semicircular dance floor called the *orchestra*. Originally, the chorus and actors were probably in the orchestra. In the Hellenistic period, the actors were on a raised platform behind the orchestra, called the *skēnē*. At that time, a back wall was erected to serve as a sounding board. Yet what the stage looked like in the fifth and fourth centuries BC, when the theater was at its peak, remains uncertain. The word *skēnē* actually means nothing other than a shed or storeroom and indicates that it originally was a small room (of wood) where the actors changed their costumes and masks. The fifteen chorus members danced in the orchestra while they

540 Greek mosaic, ca. second century BC, on which the god Dionysus rides a panther. It was found on the floor of a house on the island of Delos.

Dionysus rides a mule. This vase was painted by Nikosthenes, ca. sixth century BC.

sang or recited texts. Across from them—whether on a platform or not—the actors recited and sang the most important parts of the tragedy. With gestures, dance steps, and masks, they gave shape to the drama. The stage was only occasionally decorated. No attempt was made to make anything appear naturalistic. At the beginning of an episode, an actor or the chorus would simply set the scene. Not until Hellenistic and Roman times was it considered necessary to imitate reality.

Unlike the members of the chorus, the actors were professionals. Because no more than three actors were allowed on the stage in the tragedies, the players often had double roles. It was also necessary, on the other hand, to have one role played by more than one actor. Women were not allowed to act, although they could be members of the chorus. Female roles were played by men. All this was made possible by the use of masks. The actors also changed the timbre of their voices. The cast of the satyr play corresponded to that of the tragedy, but in the comedy, more than three (also masked) actors were used.

In fifth-century BC Athens, no pieces were performed twice. This means that every

Terra-cotta statue of a dancing actor, made in the Hellenistic period

541

year, seventeen premieres were performed. Only a very few of them were passed down in their complete state: tragedies by Aeschylus, Sophocles, and Euripides, and comedies of Aristophanes, forty-four pieces of the more than one thousand that must have been produced in the fifth century.

The Tragic Poets

In a number of cases, the content of Greek tragedies is known from primary source material: the plays themselves. Usually, however, we must make do with a few fragments or descriptions. The oldest dramatist-poet known by name is Thespis, but none of his work survives. More evidence remains of Choerilus, whose career began at the same time as that of Thespis in the sixth century and whose extant work includes a couple of small fragments and one title, *Alopé*, perhaps a satyr play. We know somewhat more of Phrynichus, who claimed a victory in the poetic competitions during the last decade of the sixth century. Among his various works,

A seat of honor
in the theater of Dionysus
in Athens,
that was built ca.
500 BC

Bust of Aeschylus
(525-456 BC),
one of the three great Attic
tragic playwrights.
Some of the seventy tragedies
he wrote are still performed
in our time, including
the *Persians*.

542

perhaps the *Capture of Miletus* is most interesting. In this piece, contemporary history—the capture of the city of Miletus by the Persians in 494 BC—was incorporated into a tragedy. These oldest tragedies consisted almost exclusively of lyrical chorus parts that were interrupted now and then by a single actor.

Aeschylus

The heyday of Greek tragedy began with the young Aeschylus, who was born around 525 BC in Eleusis. Aeschylus took part in the competition of tragedians during the Dionysia in 499 BC, but he did not win until 484 BC. Of the ninety tragedies that Aeschylus wrote, only seven have been preserved. Three of these seven tragedies form the trilogy with which Aeschylus won the Dionysian competition in Athens in 458 BC. It is the only extant trilogy. Its accompanying satyr play, the *Proteus*, has unfortunately been lost. These three are normally called the *Oresteia*, after the main character, Orestes. This trilogy, an exquisite example of Aeschylus's style at the high point of his poetic genius, was probably also his last work. He died two years after the performance in the city of Gela on Sicily.

The *Oresteia* concerns the fate of the royal family of the Atreides. The first drama, *Agamemnon*, treats the homecoming and the murder of Agamemnon, the leader of the Greeks in the Trojan War. The play takes place in the Palace of Mycenae, where the king returns to his wife Clytemnestra after many years of absence. In the interim, she has had an affair with Aegisthus. Clytemnestra hates her husband, who sacrificed their daughter Iphigenia to appease the gods. She and her lover develop a plan to kill him. Despite the warnings of the Trojan princess Cassandra, who was taken by Agamemnon as a slave from Troy, Agamemnon is killed by Clytemnestra and Aegisthus shortly after his arrival. After the murder, Clytemnestra justifies her action to the chorus:

"I am not ashamed to say that I have thrown sand in the eyes of my enemy. I feigned friendship and love—and he did not escape his fate. For many years, I cherished this desire in my heart. And now it has hap-

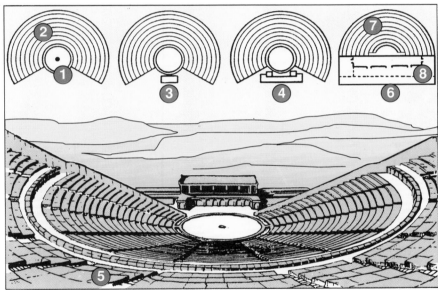

The development of the classical theater. The basic elements of Greek theater were the *orchestra* (1), surrounded by the *theatron* (2), where the audience sat. Near the *orchestra*, a *skēnē* (3) was built as a permanent background. The skēnē, on and in front of which more and more acts were played, became higher and deeper (4), as in the theater of Epidaurus (5). In the Roman theater (6) the space for the audience, the *cavea* (7), was in the form of a semicircle. The space for the players, the *podium* (8), was extended to cover almost the whole diameter of the theater.

pened! I stabbed him. Why should I deny it? I set the trap, and when he was caught in the net, I stabbed him twice. Did you not hear his cries for help? He fell on the ground, and with a third thrust of the dagger, I finished him off. He is now among the dead. I struck deep in his heart and his blood spurted upon me. I was gladdened with that red liquid which flowed over me, as the fields are gladdened when it rains."

543

The character of Clytemnestra is perfectly portrayed by Aeschylus. Her passion and her feelings of revenge dominate the course of the drama. The visionary, dreamy Cassandra and the selfish Aegisthus are beautifully brought to life.

Actor's mask
of the deified Heracles,
ca. second century BC.
Heracles was the son of Zeus
and Alcméne and famous
for his heroic deeds.

In the second drama of the trilogy, the *Libation Bearers* or *Choepheroi*, the murder of Agamemnon is avenged by his son Orestes, who kills his own mother and her lover. In the third part, the *Eumenides*, Orestes is pursued by the goddesses of vengeance, finding no peace until a special court in Athens pronounces sentence on his matricide. The voice of the goddess Athena pronounces the decision: Orestes is not guilty.

Of the four other remaining works of Aeschylus, the *Persians* relates to the Greek victory over Persia in the battle of Salamis. This event is approached from a Persian viewpoint. In Susa, the people foresee the disastrous outcome of the war. Xerxes arrives there a broken man. In *The Suppliants*, Aeschylus writes about the escape of the Danaids to Argos. King Danaus of Libya refused to marry off his fifty daughters to the fifty sons of his twin brother Aegyptus. They found refuge in Argos, but the Danaids were still forced into marriage. All but Hypermnestra, who spared her husband, proceeded to murder their brand-new husbands. With this couple, the new royal family of Argos began. The residents were henceforth called Danaoi. *Seven against Thebes* is about the fratricidal struggle between the brothers Eteocles and Polyneices for the possession of the throne of Thebes, and the battle of the Seven Heroes for possession of this city. *Prometheus Bound* portrays the story of Prometheus, demigod and friend of man. He gave fire to mankind in defiance of Zeus, who punished him by chaining him to a rock, where an eagle tore at his liver every day. In almost all of Aeschylus's dramas, the principal theme is that man must yield to the jealous power of the gods, who in turn are subject to a higher power: fate.

Sophocles

The successor and, for some time, also the competitor of Aeschylus, was Sophocles. He was almost thirty years younger and came from an old, noble family in Athens. In addition to his popularity as a poet, Sophocles was one of the ten Athenian *stratēgoi*, or generals, of the year 440 BC, together with Pericles. Sophocles's literary career began in 468 BC, when he took part for the first time in the Dionysian competition and defeated Aeschylus. He won another eighteen times. Although Sophocles was the most popular tragedian of Athens, only 7 of the estimated 123 tragedies remain.

Less convinced of the unchangeability of fate than Aeschylus, Sophocles gave greater play to human will. The consequences of attempting to alter one's fate, however, could be tragic. This heightens dramatic tension. In many ways, Sophocles was an innovator. He was the dramatist who introduced the third actor on the stage, a convention later taken over by Aeschylus. He also broke with the tradition that the tragedian himself must act in his own pieces, as Aeschylus still did.

None of Sophocles's trilogies remain. The seven well-known tragedies are all independent works in their own right: *Ajax*, *Antigone*, *Electra*, *Oedipus Rex*, *Trachiniai*, *Philoctetes*, and *Oedipus at Colonus*. (There is also a large part of a satyr play he wrote, called the *Sleuth Hounds*.)

In *Antigone*, Sophocles examines the conflict between human laws and natural (or divine) laws. Antigone is a daughter of Oedipus who shares the old king's banishment. Her brothers, Eteocles and Polyneices, fight over the throne of Thebes. Both die in a battle before the gates of that city. The kingship now falls to their mother's brother, Creon. He strictly forbids Antigone to bury the body of her brother Polyneices, a traitor to his country. The body would have to lie dishonored on the battlefield as prey to the dogs and vultures. Antigone takes no notice of her uncle's order. The only thing that matters to her is the moral obligation to give her dead brother a fitting burial, so that his ghost will have rest. Creon abides by his threats and has the girl walled-up alive in a tomb. Even the passionate pleas of his son Haemon, who is in love with Antigone, cannot sway him from his decision. Desperate, Haemon hurries to the tomb to save his loved one, against his father's orders. But he arrives too late; Antigone has already hung herself. Now fate steps in, as Haemon also kills himself. When Creon returns to his palace with the biers of Antigone and his son, he hears that his wife has also taken her own life. Creon remains behind, a broken and despairing man. Sophocles directs all his attention to the conflict in the human soul: Antigone, Haemon, but also Creon, are torn

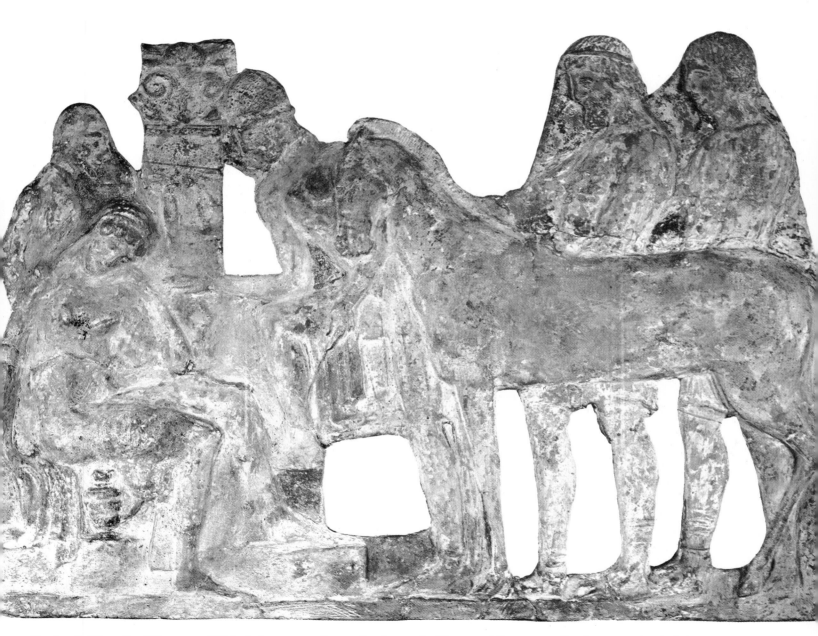

Greek relief from the fifth century BC depicting a scene from a Greek tragedy. Electra and Orestes stand at the grave of their father, Agamemnon, the king of Mycenae who led the Greeks in the war against Troy.

Marble statue of Sophocles, Aeschylus's competitor and successor and the most popular tragedian-poet of Athens. During his life (496–406 BC) he wrote over 120 tragedies, some of which have survived and are still staged today.

him as the most modern of the Greek tragedians, primarily because of the extensive development of his characters. They are far more realistic and human in quality than those of his fellow playwrights. *Medea* is the enchantress known in Greek mythology for helping Jason gain the golden fleece and for repeatedly resorting to murder to attain her ends. *Medea* illustrates Euripides's rare sympathetic portrayal of women. In *Hippolytus*, Phaedra falls in love with her stepson Hippolytus. As a punishment for Hippolytus, who has angered Aphrodite, the goddess has sparked this love, which horrifies the chaste youth. Phaedra commits suiside, but leaves a note accusing Hippolytus of lusting after her. The end is tragic for all.

The Comic Poets

Aristophanes, one of the great comic poets of what is called the Old Comedy of Greek literature, ridiculed Euripides and Aeschylus in the *Frogs*. His first work, entitled *Daitaleis* (the *Revellers*), produced in 427 BC, no longer survives. He roundly satirized Socrates as the master of a school that trains students in false rhetoric in the *Clouds*.

Aristophanes bridged the distance into the later category of Greek comic plays called Middle Comedy from about 400 to 336 BC. (These eras are defined by critics in terms of the style of comedy used by their various authors.) Aristophanes is the only Old Comedy dramatist whose work survives in more than fragments. An enormously popular dramatist in his time, Aristophanes was supremely comic in his parodies of politicians such as the demagogue Cleon, taking advantage of the unprecedented freedom of speech, marking Athenian democracy. He is the author of *Lysistrata*, *The Frogs*, *Plutus*, and many others.

In the New Comedy of Menander and others writing between 336 and 250 BC, virtually no satire is seen. Social comedy took over the stage in much the same way as it has television. Theater pieces dealt with family situations, highlighting individual characters, their foibles, and their various loves.

between human and natural laws. It is precisely because of Sophocles's emphasis on psychological problems that *Antigone* is regarded as one of the great works of all time. The problems it treats are as current today as they were then. Like the third prominent tragedian, Euripides, Sophocles was very psychologically astute.

Euripides

Euripides, like Aeschylus, a younger contemporary of Sophocles, wrote some ninety-two plays. Of these, eighteen tragedies (one of which is of doubtful origin) and one satyr play (*The Cyclops*) remain. Many critics see

The Basilica, a Doric temple dedicated to Hera. It was built in the sixth century BC in the Greek colony Poseidonia (later called Paestum) in Campania (southern Italy).

From Pythagoras to Diogenes

Two Centuries of Greek Thinking

The foundation of much of western scientific thought was laid in the Ionian cities of Asia Minor. Thales, Anaximander, and Anaximenes represented three generations of pre-Socratic philosophy in what came to be called the School of Miletus. They were the first to separate science from mythology, although they did not entirely abandon the conceptual universe of the latter. These philosophers attempted to explain natural phenomena on the basis of their own perceptions and independent consideration, without recourse to previous thinking. One of the results of the Persian drive into Asia Minor was the emigration of Ionian scholars to the Greek mainland and its colonies.

Anaxagoras (ca. 500-428) was born about 500 BC in Clazomenae and he moved to Athens about 480 BC, the first of many philosophers to do so. In contrast to earlier thinkers who had looked to earth, air, fire, and water for the origin of ultimate reality, Anaxagoras presented the doctrines of *nous* (later adopted by Aristotle, it meant eternal intelligence, from the Greek for "mind" or "reason"). In his writings *Peri Physeos* (*On*

Nature), only portions of which remain, he suggested that all matter had existed in a state of chaos as infinitely numerous and small particles. Order, he postulated, was produced out of chaos by nous.

Anaxagoras taught in Athens for some thirty years. His students included the dramatist Euripides and possibly Socrates.

His friend, the statesman Pericles, was of little help to him when he was sent to prison for insisting that the stars, including the sun itself, were glowing masses of hot stone and that the moon receives its light from the sun. This teaching was far ahead of its time. Banished from Athens, Anaxagoras retired to Lampsacus, on the Asiatic shore of the Hellespont, where he died in 428 BC.

Pythagoras

The flow of thinkers out of Ionia resulted in schools in southern Italy, on Sicily, and in Athens. One of the most important representatives of these new schools was Pythagoras, born about 582 BC on the island of Samos, off the coast of Asia Minor. Apparently unhappy with the policies of the tyrant Polycrates, he left Samos for southern Italy, settling in Croton about 530 BC.

Pythagoras and his mystical brotherhood of followers formed a religious-philosophical sect, distinguished by a combination of numeric mysticism with mathematical knowledge, as well as a theory regarding life after death, and a strongly ascetic attitude. Their doctrine of *metempsychosis*, or the passing of the soul at death into another body, either human or animal, may have stemmed from Iranian and even Indian religion. Ionia was certainly open to many influences from the East.

The sectarian character of the movement of the Pythagoreans must be emphasized. It marks one of the first times in the comparatively formless Greek religion that a group distinguishes itself as a sect. One story told is that the residents of Croton distrusted the sect and set fire to its building around 500 BC. The bitter Pythagoras then left for Metapontion, where he died somewhere early in the fifth century BC. At a later stage, the Pythagoreans apparently gave up their role as improvers of the world and retreated into a sort of monastic community. Until the fourth century, the Pythagoreans remained as a community in Tarentum in southern Italy. Later, individual Pythagoreans fanned out throughout the Greek world. It seems they had a great influence. Aristotle, for example, was interested in their concepts.

The ideas of Pythagoras can be summarized in three points. First there is the concept of purity and *askēsis* (training, or exercise). He who does not succeed in keeping

Black-figured Attic amphora, made by Exedias, ca. 550–530 BC. Ajax and Achilles are playing a board game.

548

his body pure by following the rules of life also contaminates his soul. Unjust behavior also pollutes the soul. The tarnished soul is not capable of *sophia* (wisdom, or knowledge and insight). Through one's conduct in life, one can affect one's character and eternal fate for better or for worse. This is expressed in the rebirth of the soul: a wrongful life can lead to reincarnation as an animal. (Pythagoras apparently claimed memory of a previous life as the Trojan War soldier Euphorbus.) The goal is to attain as much sophia as possible; through this pursuit, the soul rises toward a better body in the next life; possessing sophia makes the soul equal to god. There seemed to be no desire, as in Buddhism, to break through the series of reincarnations.

Pythagoras searched for patterns, teaching that the essence of all things lay in numbers and that all relationships could be expressed numerically. They saw a numerical relationship in musical notes. The Pythagorean concept of numbers formed the ultimate principle of all proportion, order, and harmony in the universe. Skilled mathematicians,

Pythagoreans influenced early Euclidian geometry. The Pythagorean theorem of geometry states that the square of the hypotenuse (the diagonal line) of a right tri-

The Temple of Concordia (this is the traditional name since it is unsure to which deity this temple was dedicated) in Agrigento, Sicily. It is a Doric temple, built ca. 430 BC.

Bust, made in the third century BC, of Parmenides of Elea, a famous Greek philosopher (515-451 BC)

549

The so-called Temple of
Castor and Pollux,
a reconstruction made
in AD 1836,
in which parts of
different fifth-
century BC buildings
were put together.
The building stands
on the temple field near
Agrigento (Sicily).

Marble head
of the philosopher Plato
(427-347 BC)
made in Greece ca.
340 BC

550

angle is equal to the sum of the squares of the other two sides.

Pythagoreans were among the first to teach that the earth is a spherical planet revolving around a fixed point. They saw a numerical scheme behind the harmonious arrangement of even the heavenly bodies. These they considered separated from each other by intervals that corresponded to the harmonic lengths of strings. The very movement of the heavenly bodies, they contended, produced music, the "harmony of the spheres." This *harmonia* (harmony) was universal, prevailing everywhere.

Pythagoreans attributed an ethical value to numbers themselves. Maintaining purity through ascesis, searching for insight along the way of rebirths, and attaining knowledge of the harmony that pervades the world were closely interconnected concepts.

The School of Elea

Pythagoras exercised a profound influence on a great many Greek thinkers of the fifth century BC, not all of whom can be called Pythagoreans. Many of them built their theories on his pioneering work rather than seeking to elaborate on it. One of these philosophers was Parmenides from Elea, a small Greek colony south of Naples. Parmenides was possibly a student of Xenophanes, but indicated that he had "converted to a contemplative life" through Pythagorean thought.

Parmenides expressed his ideas in the form of a didactic poem, large parts of which remain. He assumes that all movement— exchange and change—is nothing other than outward appearance. Only "being" exists; there is no "not being." For Parmenides, being and thinking represent the same thing. The "being" is like a sphere: perfect on all sides, indivisible, unchangeable, immovable, unborn, and imperishable. The newness in Parmenides's theory is evident if you compare him to the great Ionian philosophers of the seventh and sixth centuries BC. They presupposed that all things were derived from a basic element, whether that was water, fire, air, or earth. They assumed that the contraction of fire, air, or water brought about changes in nature. But in order to become concentrated, matter must enclose more matter within its mass and, therefore, occupy a place that was originally empty. This vacuum is what Parmenides called "not being." Because he believed that this vacuum could not exist, he considered the entire

Statue, probably of Niobe,
dating from the second half
of the fifth century

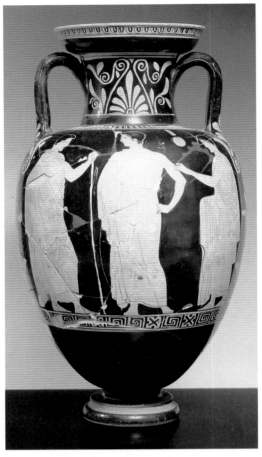

natural philosophy of the Ionian school invalid.

Neither is it impossible to explain motion in a philosophic manner. He said, when an object moves from one place to another, something must be moved that was there before, or the object has to move to a place where there was nothing. Even when one assumes that the object moves to a place where there was nothing, then the moved object must still replace another object, until such time as the object comes to a stop on a place where there was nothing. And that is impossible. "Not being"—the vacuum—simply does not exist; and consequently, neither does motion, from a philosophical viewpoint.

A student of Parmenides's, Zeno from Elea, tried to prove this theory of the "indivisibility of being" by means of a number of paradoxes. These remarkable arguments kept the attention of Greek thinking for a long time, because with all their logic, they were so totally absurd. One of Zeno's famous paradoxes is the story of Achilles and the turtle. Achilles, the fastest runner of all Greeks, challenges a turtle, the slowest of all animals, to race against him. He gives the turtle a long head start, and then they start to run at the same time. When Achilles comes to the place where the turtle had started, the turtle has run a certain distance. Achilles keeps running, but each time he arrives at the place where the turtle was, the turtle has also run a certain distance farther. As fast as Achilles runs, and as slowly as the turtle crawls, there will always be a distance for Achilles yet to cover. In other words, Achilles can never catch up to the turtle. This is the assumption of infinite divisibility. On the basis of such clever absurdities, which appealed enormously to the Greeks, Zeno attempted to demonstrate the indivisibility of being and thus that Parmenides was right.

Another of Parmenides's students was Leucippus, the founder of the theory of atoms. In Greek, the word *atomos* literally means "something which is not divisible." Leucippus posited that indeed—as Parmenides had said—there is one matter, but this matter is divided into tiny countless particles, or atoms. Each atom has volume and all atoms are equal in essence. Consequently, the diversity of things originates from the position of the combination of atoms. The point over which Leucippus stumbled was the fact that he had to allow for empty space or a vacuum between the atoms. He called that vacuum "pores between the atoms," but once again, a conflict between various philosophical trends came to light. The work of Leucippus was continued by his student Democritus from Abdera, who perfected the theory of atoms. Visible reality is made up of atoms, which are in eternal motion in endless space. Atoms are unchangeable but infinitely varied and they form, through joining together, all living and nonliving matter.

Greek thinking in the sixth and fifth centuries BC was characterized by questions that were actually unsolvable by the philosophers. Some of these concerned the structure of matter and the cause of motion. While seeking answers, a few of the philosophers discovered mathematical and scientific truths of great consequence. Such questions also gave rise to just as many misconceptions and cheap solutions, but it was the questioning itself, the reasoning, that was of greatest significance.

Sophists

Despite their importance in the development of Western thought, the philosophers so far discussed did not have the social influence of the fifth-century Sophists. The majority of the teachers who offered higher education (in classical Athens, it was always private) are termed *sophists*. The Greek word *sophistēs* (expert, master craftsman, man of wisdom), was originally applied to learned men, but it eventually took on an ugly connotation.

The negative image took root because some Sophists furthered relative thinking, looking at matters from all sides and, if necessary, defending all viewpoints. They stressed the very useful art of rhetoric, which could offer a path to success in public life. Hence, a Sophist came to be considered someone who was very handy with words, who could convince the unsuspecting listener of just about anything. Good or bad, the Sophist could make a good argument.

Sophists, quite popular in Athens at first, eventually drew fire from the philosophers Socrates, Plato, and Aristotle, and the state itself, for their indifferent morality. Plato and Aristotle criticized them for taking money, although most earned their living as itinerant teachers selling education for a fee. The term *sophist* acquired derogatory meaning, similar to the word *sophistry*, defined as deceptive or false reasoning. On one occasion, Socrates compared the Sophist to a fisherman. Both try to fish—one to catch his meal, the other to catch people and cheat them out of their money in exchange for false teachings.

Socrates (ca. 470-ca. 399 BC)

Socrates was of low origin, unlike most of the philosophers, the son of the sculptor Sophroniscus and Phaenarete, a midwife. It is not known who his teachers were, but he seems to have been acquainted with the doctrines of Parmenides, Heraclitus, and Anaxagoras. There is no clear indication as

to how Socrates supported himself. He apparently worked as a sculptor for a while. His statue of the three Graces stood near the entrance to the Acropolis until the second century AD. He fought as a hoplite for Athens in the Peloponnesian War, serving

Bust of Democritus (ca. 460–370 BC). This bronze statue is a Roman copy of an original (ca. 250 BC) and was found in Herculaneum.

Bust of Antisthenes, one of Socrates's pupils, made in the third century BC

553

A centaur, a creature with a human torso and a horse's hindquarters and legs, snatches a maenad (devotee of Dionysus). This scene is depicted on a relief of the Parthenon that was built in 447-432 BC.

with distinction in the battle of Potidaea in 432-430 BC. His wife was named Xanthippe; they had three children.

He evidently turned that otherwise normal life into one of public dialogue in the marketplaces and squares of Athens out of a sense of calling. He wanted to be a philosopher, to guide the moral and intellectual improvement of Athens. He wrote no books

and established no formal school of philosophy. What is known about him and his thinking comes primarily from the works of his student Plato who, in turn, had Aristotle as a student, and, to a lesser extent, from the fourth-century historian Xenophon. It is through their writings that Socrates exerted his profound effect on all later Western thinking.

Socrates rejected the battle of philosophic ideas of the "one," the "indivisible" or the "eternally changeable," and refused to become involved in the search for the "core of things" or "basic matter." His interest was in rational argument and general definition. He was essentially an ethical philosopher. He was interested in the objective understanding of love, justice, and virtue (defined as knowledge). He contended that all vice was the result of ignorance, that no one was intentionally bad. Since those who know what is right will act rightly, virtue is knowledge.

Socrates ridiculed the Sophists and the rhetoricians. He was unrelenting in employing logic as a weapon in his philosophic duels. In these "battles," clarity and clearness of expression had the highest priority. To express metaphysical truth, he used expressions and terms directly derived from daily life. He despised and rejected rhetoric, long-winded arguments about nothing. Socrates did not wish to speak but to think. Plato gives us an image of the manner in which Socrates managed to totally embarrass one of the most famous Sophists of Athens, Gorgias, simply by continuing to ask questions. He could have made it difficult for Protagoras as well.

In one of Plato's *Dialogues*, a conversation between Socrates and the great philosophers of Elea, Parmenides and Zeno, is beautifully illustrated. The two philosophers had come to Athens to attend the Panathenaea and stayed in the home of Plato's stepbrother. One morning Socrates visits the famous guests and stirs their passions. Parmenides kindly answers Socrates's questions, while Zeno does his best to get the troublesome questioner out the door.

Socrates sums up his impression of the two philosophers very succinctly: "I understand that Zeno is actually a second Parmenides, even though he says things in a totally different manner. You, Parmenides, want to convince us that everything is one, and Zeno says, on the other hand, that diversity cannot exist. So you argue in two different manners to express the truth: one of you claims something, and the other repudiates the opposite. Something like this presupposes a mental effort which far exceeds my moderate abilities."

Socrates's attitude toward the two philosophers from Elea illustrates his manner of thinking. He typically presented himself as someone who needed things explained to him. This profession of ignorance, given his brilliance and extraordinary ability to define the sides of any argument, is called Socratic irony.

In the manner of the Athenian Sophists, Socrates wanted to place man at the center of his considerations, but he fiercely rejected their negative attitude. Only the good can be a guide for the behavior of man; man must strive toward knowing that good. When he has found that out, he will pursue it; no one will ever deliberately go against good. Socrates established his philosophic inquiries in the form of a conversation or dialogue. Starting from the specific, he sought general truths through an endless game of question and answer. Socrates also accepted something like "the voice of one's

Bust of Heraclitus of Ephesus, a famous philosopher who lived from ca. 549 to 480 BC

555

Engraving from the
18th century, depicting Diogenes
who, sitting in his cask,
meets the famous Macedonian
general Alexander the Great.
According to the legend,
the philosopher asked
Alexander to step out of
his sunlight.

conscience," an instinctive, nonrational sense of higher values that could keep man from committing wrongful actions.

In his daily life Socrates contrasted sharply with the Sophists. He refused to gather paying students around him. He presented questions to anyone talking with him at any given time. He elicited answers which, through sharp analysis mixed with mild derision, he then rejected as inadequate or incorrect. He then attempted to reach a logical and correct conclusion, together with his "victim", on the basis of clear-cut definitions. The goal, of course, was hardly ever

achieved, but the value of the discussion lay in the enlightenment of both participants.

In 399 BC, Socrates, although both a patriot who had served his country in battle and a man who had strong religious convictions, was charged with religious heresies and corrupting the morals of Athenian youth. His criticism of the Sophists and of Athenian

Bust of Socrates,
the famous Greek philosopher
who lived from 469 to
399 BC. One of his pupils
was Plato. ❯

political and religious institutions made him many enemies. He was burlesqued by the dramatist Aristophanes in the *Clouds*, as the director of a "thinking shop." It is now believed that his arrest stemmed from the influence on Alcibiades and Critias, who were hated by those in power in Athens, which was in crisis and hostile to nonconformity.

Athenian law determined that the accused had to defend himself by means of a public speech. We have two versions of Socrates's defending arguments. Both attest to his beautiful ironic style and his simple dialectic. In Plato's *Apology*, Socrates disputed the Athenian judges' authority to sentence him to death, as the accusers wished, with the same frank arguments he once used with the Sophists. He pointed out great gaps in the official accusation. He had clearly determined that if they took offense at his life and work, then they had to condemn him. He could never deny what he had asserted for so many years. Socrates could have avoided his heavy sentence by using a different defense, based less deeply on principle. Had he done so, he would have gotten off with a fine, and there were enough students who would have only been too happy to pay it for him. He was condemned to die, although at first only by a small majority. When Socrates countered, as allowed under Athenian law, with an ironic proposition to change the death sentence to a small fine because his importance to the state was also small, the enraged jury voted again, increasing the majority for death.

Socrates could easily have fled; friends even planned his escape. He preferred to comply with the verdict and die. Plato's *Phaedo* describes his final day with friends and admirers. In the evening, in accordance with the usual method of execution, he drank the cup of hemlock, made from a poisonous herb.

The Cynics

Some of Socrates's students attempted to put his views into practice, making ethics the center of their thinking and planning their lifestyles around the philosophical concepts they considered essential. Socrates's example influenced them to take direct action. This fact is more important than the specific content of their philosophy.

One of these students was Antisthenes, a founder of the Cynics. He was a Sophist until influenced by Socrates to protest against the material interests of established society. He contended that people must free themselves from all needs; that only striving toward the good could offer a happy life. Any form of luxury or pleasure made people slaves and, therefore, unhappy.

These ideas were elaborated upon to the extreme by Diogenes from Sinope. As a young man he went to Athens and became a student of Antisthenes. He brought the ideal of poverty and austerity into practice with Socratic consistency, founding the Cynic School. Plato was once said to have called him "Socrates gone mad." Diogenes rejected all social conventions. This earned him the abusive name *kuon*, "cur or dog," the nickname of his followers, the *kunikoi*, or Cynics. Holding virtue to be the only good, they stressed independence from worldly needs and pleasures and led austere lives.

A Doric temple, built in the late sixth century BC. It was probably dedicated to Hera and built just outside the Greek colony Metapontum.

Attic red-figured *pelikē* (special type of amphora) from ca. 450 BC, on which Dionysus is surrounded by satyrs and maenads

TIME LINE

THE GREEK WORLD POLITICAL HISTORY	THE GREEK WORLD CULTURAL HISTORY	EVENTS IN THE REST OF THE WORLD
		ca. 1500 Earliest evidence for alphabet in Western Levant
		1361-1352 Tutankhamen is pharaoh of Egypt
BC		
1200 **ca. 1200** Decline of the Mycenaean palaces; the late Mycenaean period		**ca. 1200** Hittite Empire collapses
1175		
1150		
1125		**ca. 1000** Phoenician alphabet evolves
1100		**ca. 1111-256/5** Zhou Dynasty in China
1075		
1050 **ca. 1050** Beginning of the Dark Age, emergence of the city-states	**ca. 1050** Impoverishment and decline of population; writing and complex societies disappear **ca. 1050-750** Emergence of aristocracy	
1025		
1000		
975		
950 **ca. 950** Plain of Eurotas conquered by Dorian Greeks		**ca. 925-587** Kingdom of Judah in Palestine
925		
900	**ca. 900-800** Population growth; restoration of trade and contacts with the East, end of temporary isolation **ca. 900-700** Creation of Spartan form of government with dual kingship, warriors, helots, and free residents	
875		
850		
825		
800	**ca. 800** Certain Greek sanctuaries, like Delphi, become (inter)national shrines	**814** Foundation of Carthage
775		
750 **ca. 750-600** Orientalizing period	**ca. 750** Development of export industry in Corinth, Corinthian pottery, reintroduction of writing	**753** Foundation of Rome by Romulus

Prehistory	Antiquity	Middle Ages	Renaissance	Modern History	Contemporary History

THE GREEK WORLD POLITICAL HISTORY	THE GREEK WORLD CULTURAL HISTORY	EVENTS IN THE REST OF THE WORLD

BC

750

ca. 750-550 Archaic colonization; foundation of coastal settlements on the Mediterranean and the Black Seas; emergence of new independent states
ca. 750-500 Archaic period, power in the hands of the aristocracy
ca. 750 Corinth develops into the foremost port and the most prosperous town in Greece

ca. 750-700 Composition of the Homeric epics, the *Iliad* and *Odyssey*
c.750-550 Newly founded colonies adopt the culture, religion, forms of government, and dialect of the mother cities; colonization due to lack of land, economic necessity, and politics; dissemination of Greek culture over a large area of the Black Sea
ca. 750-500 Agriculture is the foundation of the economy; landed property commands respect

ca. 722-705 Reign of Sargon II; construction of royal city Dur-Sharrukin (Khorsabad)

ca. 700-600 Etruscans adopt the Greek alphabet

700

ca. 700 Conquest of Messenia by Sparta; Athens is governed by nine archons of aristocratic descent
ca.700 Lycurgus, who may be legendary, gives laws to Sparta; Spartan society develops
ca. 700-600 Social tension at every level of society creates unrest

ca. 675 Ionians from Colophon found a colony at Siris in south Italy

ca. 700 Mysteries play major role in Greek religion; wealth expressed in bronze weapons
ca. 700-600 Poetry is no longer bound to traditional epic forms
ca. 700-500 Under Greek influence, a Mediterranean urban culture develops in central Italy; growth of overseas trade

ca. 660 Legendary founding of Japan

650

ca. 650 In Corinth, the ruling Bacchiad dynasty is ousted by the tyrant Cypselus, who continues the policies that ensure prosperity
ca. 650-500 Tyranny becomes the most prevalent type of government in the Greek world, undermines the position of the aristocracy, and clears the way for democracy

ca. 650 Poet Tyrtaeus composes marching songs and battle hymns; Archilochus and Semonides write iambic poetry
ca. 650-500 Tyrants popular with the nonaristocratic population

ca. 625 Alcman composes lyric poetry for choirs

612 Beginning of the Neo-Babylonian Empire

600

594-593 Through legal reform, Solon ends the worst abuses of Athenian law, including enslavement of debtors

ca. 600-550 Thales of Miletus is the first-known Ionian natural philosopher; Arion composes the first Dionysian hymn not devoted to the god Dionysus
ca. 600-500 Spartan society becomes rigid, stagnant, and conservative
ca. 600 Minted coins; lyricists Alcaeus of Mytilene and Sappho of Lésvos; mysteries of Eleusis

ca. 600 Foundation of Teotihuacán

586 The Jews in Babylonian captivity

580

Prehistory	Antiquity	Middle Ages	Renaissance	Modern History	Contemporary History

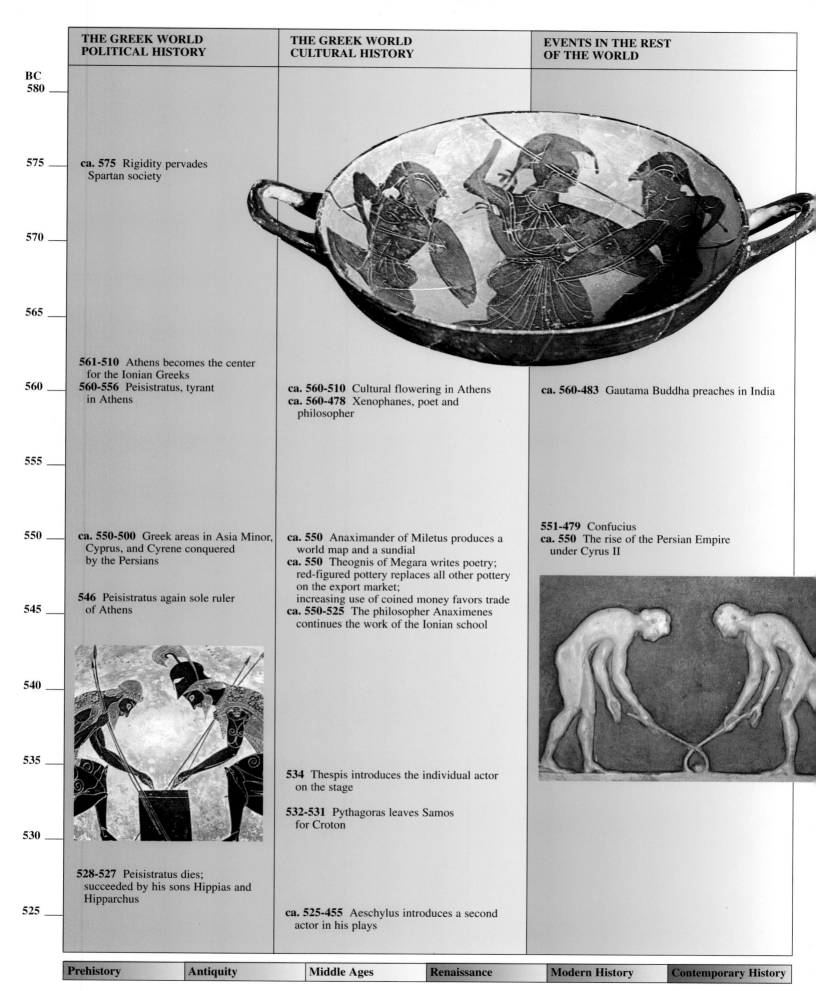

THE GREEK WORLD POLITICAL HISTORY	THE GREEK WORLD CULTURAL HISTORY	EVENTS IN THE REST OF THE WORLD

BC

580

575   **ca. 575** Rigidity pervades Spartan society

570

565

560   **561-510** Athens becomes the center for the Ionian Greeks
560-556 Peisistratus, tyrant in Athens

ca. 560-510 Cultural flowering in Athens
ca. 560-478 Xenophanes, poet and philosopher

ca. 560-483 Gautama Buddha preaches in India

555

550   **ca. 550-500** Greek areas in Asia Minor, Cyprus, and Cyrene conquered by the Persians

ca. 550 Anaximander of Miletus produces a world map and a sundial
ca. 550 Theognis of Megara writes poetry; red-figured pottery replaces all other pottery on the export market; increasing use of coined money favors trade
ca. 550-525 The philosopher Anaximenes continues the work of the Ionian school

551-479 Confucius
ca. 550 The rise of the Persian Empire under Cyrus II

545   **546** Peisistratus again sole ruler of Athens

540

535   **534** Thespis introduces the individual actor on the stage

532-531 Pythagoras leaves Samos for Croton

530

525   **528-527** Peisistratus dies; succeeded by his sons Hippias and Hipparchus

ca. 525-455 Aeschylus introduces a second actor in his plays

Prehistory	Antiquity	Middle Ages	Renaissance	Modern History	Contemporary History

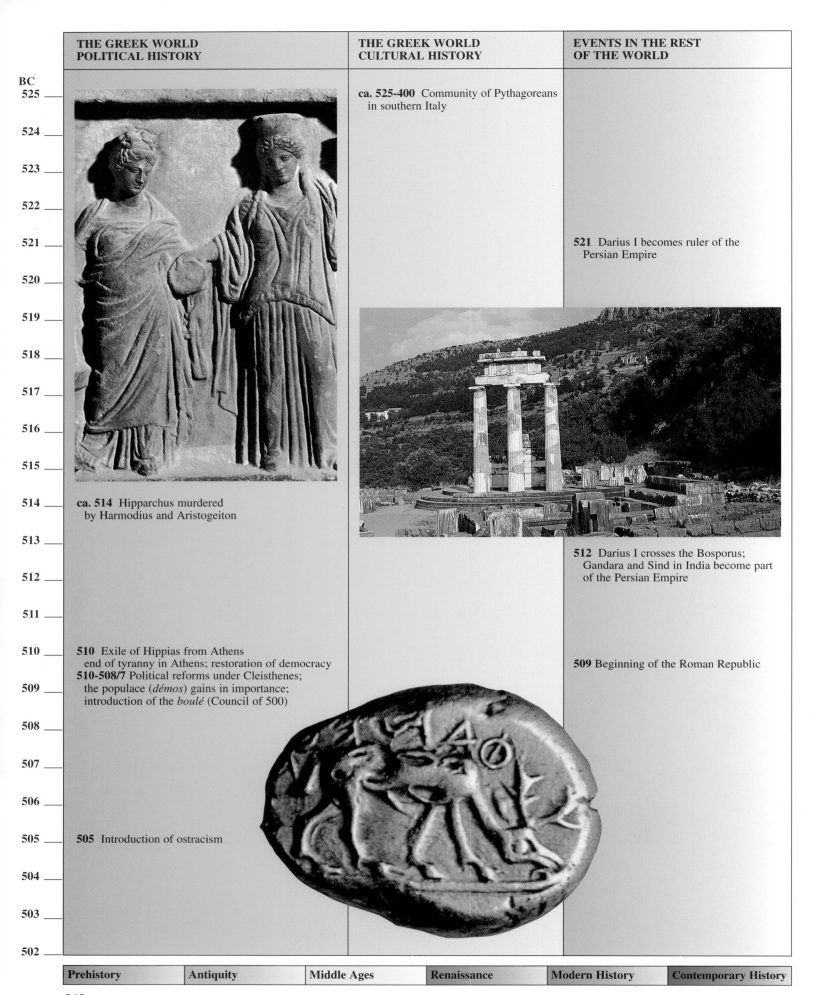

THE GREEK WORLD POLITICAL HISTORY	THE GREEK WORLD CULTURAL HISTORY	EVENTS IN THE REST OF THE WORLD

BC

ca. 525-400 Community of Pythagoreans in southern Italy

521 Darius I becomes ruler of the Persian Empire

ca. 514 Hipparchus murdered by Harmodius and Aristogeiton

512 Darius I crosses the Bosporus; Gandara and Sind in India become part of the Persian Empire

510 Exile of Hippias from Athens end of tyranny in Athens; restoration of democracy
510-508/7 Political reforms under Cleisthenes; the populace (*démos*) gains in importance; introduction of the *boulé* (Council of 500)

509 Beginning of the Roman Republic

505 Introduction of ostracism

Prehistory	Antiquity	Middle Ages	Renaissance	Modern History	Contemporary History

BC	THE GREEK WORLD POLITICAL HISTORY	THE GREEK WORLD CULTURAL HISTORY	EVENTS IN THE REST OF THE WORLD
502			
501	ca. 500 Approximately 6,000 men constitute the Athenian popular assembly (*ecclesia*); male citizens participate collectively in the city administration	ca. 500 The word *demos* encompasses all citizens; as soldiers, helots may obtain the status of freemen; death of Spartan poetry;	ca. 500 Strike by the Roman plebeians; institution of the *concilium plebis*
500	ca. 500-400 Generals play a major role in Athenian political decisions; populace both approves and criticizes Athenian democracy	contribution of trade to the entire economy is limited; Persian naval power threatens the trade position of the Greek cities	
499	499 Ionian uprising against Persian domination	ca. 500-400 Flowering of Greek tragedy with dramatists such as Aeschylus, Sophocles, and Euripides	
498		ca. 500-428 Anaxagoras, a natural philosopher	
497		497-405 Sophocles, a writer of tragedies	
496			
495	495 Greeks lose a major naval battle with the Persians off the coast of Asia Minor	ca. 495-445 Zeno of Elea	
494			
493		493 Destruction of Miletus by the Persians	493 Rome joins the Latin League
492	492 Annexation of Thrace and Macedonia into the Persian Empire		
491	491 Persian king demands submission of the Greek city-states; Athens and Sparta refuse		
490	490 Persian expedition against Greece; Greek victory at Marathon strengthens will to resist		
489	490-480 Under Themistocles, Athens becomes a naval power		
488			
487	487 Athenian archons no longer chosen by election, but by lot		
486			486 Darius dies and is succeeded by Xerxes
485		ca. 485-406 Euripides, a writer of tragedies	
484		ca. 485-415 Protagoras, philosopher, one of the most famous of the Sophists	
483		ca. 484-424 Herodotus, Greek historian	
482	482 Persuaded by Themistocles, Athens invests the high proceeds from its silver mines to build a fleet		
481			481 Persians make new plans for the conquest of Greece
480	480 Battle of Thermopylae; death of the Spartan king Leonidas; Sparta claims military hegemony; destruction of Athens by Xerxes; Greeks win battle of Salamis		

Prehistory	Antiquity	Middle Ages	Renaissance	Modern History	Contemporary History

563

THE GREEK WORLD POLITICAL HISTORY	THE GREEK WORLD CULTURAL HISTORY	EVENTS IN THE REST OF THE WORLD

BC

480

479 Persians try to persuade Athens to accept peace; victories for the Greeks at battles of Plataea and Cape Mycale

478-477 Foundation of the Delian League against Persia, led by Athens

478

476

474

472

470

468

466

464 Rebellion of the helots in Messenia

462 Power of the Athenian Areopagus curtailed

460-429 Pericles active as general and orator

458

456

454

452

450 — ca. 450 *Ecclesia* meets ten times annually; league treasury is moved from Delos to Athens; Athenian dominance; peace with Persia; nonaristocrats emerge as leading orators (demagogues) of the Athenian popular assembly

448

446

444

443 Athens founds the colony of Thurii in southern Italy

442

440

---

479 High point of Athenian culture and art; Athens is an open society with power and wealth

ca. 470-399 Socrates

ca. 460-400 Thucydides writes histories with no mention of divine influence

ca. 460-370 Democritus continues the work of his teacher Leucippus

458 The *Oresteia* of Aeschylus

ca. 453 Hippocrates searches for natural explanations of diseases

ca. 450 Tribute from Delian League increases the prosperity of Athens

ca. 450-385 Aristophanes, author of comedies

447-406 Reconstruction of the Acropolis

ca. 445-360 Antisthenes, founder of the Cynics

440 Sophocles and Pericles are designated among the ten generals

429-347 Plato

ca. 400-325 Diogenes, founder of the Cynics

399 Socrates tried and condemned to death

384-322 Aristotle

ca. 350 Xenophon, Athenian historian

ca. 150 Compilation of definitive text of the *Iliad* and the *Odyssey*

480-221 Period of the warring states in China

474 Last great attack of the Etruscans repelled by the Latins

ca. 450 The Laws of the Twelve Tables in Rome

Prehistory	Antiquity	Middle Ages	Renaissance	Modern History	Contemporary History

Glossary

Achaea old name for Greece; the region inhabited by the descendants of Achaeus. According to Greek mythology, Achaeus was the grandson of Hellen, the legendary ancestor of the Hellenes, or Greeks.

Achaeans collective name used by Homer in his epics, the *Iliad* and the *Odyssey*, for the people of ancient Greece.

Achilles Greek hero of the Trojan War.

acropolis fortified elevated part of an ancient Greek city. The most famous fortress is the Acropolis in Athens, where various large temples were built, including the Parthenon.

Aeolic Greek dialect spoken in northeastern and central Greece, on the island of Lésvos and in the north and west coast of Asia Minor.

Aeschylus (ca. 525–456 BC) Greek tragedian. Seven of his tragedies remain, including the trilogy *Oresteia* and the *Persians*. He introduced the second actor.

agora public square; political, cultural, and commercial center of the Greek city.

Alcaeus (ca. 600 BC) lyric poet from Lésvos.

alphabet set of written symbols representing separate spoken sounds.

amphora vase with handles.

Anaxagoras (ca. 500–428 BC) Greek philosopher whose doctrines on *nous* (eternal intelligence) and the atom had great impact on later Greek philosophy.

Anaximander (sixth century BC) Ionian natural philosopher from Miletus.

Anaximenes (585–525 BC) Ionian natural philosopher from Miletus.

apella Spartan meeting of all adult men with civil rights.

Aphrodite Greek goddess of love and beauty, daughter of Zeus.

apoikia Greek colony established as an independent settlement.

Apollo Greek god of the sun, oracles, music, poetry, and justice; son of Zeus. The god of medicine, he could also inflict disease as punishment.

Arcado Cyprian Greek dialect spoken in Arcadia (central Peloponnisos) and on Cyprus.

Archaic period the era in Greek history from about 750 to 500 BC. Named for a concept drawn from Greek art history.

Archaic colonization the establishment of settlements on the coasts of the Mediterranean and Black Seas from about 750 through the mid-sixth century BC.

Archilochus (ca. 650 BC) Greek poet and satirist from the island of Paros.

archons magistrates in Athens, beginning about the seventh century BC; elected annually. Their duties comprised legislation, justice, religion, and military affairs. After the reforms of Cleisthenes, they were selected by lot.

Areopagus the *Areos Pagos* (hill of the god Ares) next to the Athenian Acropolis, where the council of ex-archons of the same name were seated from the seventh century on.

aryballos oil flask.

askēsis (purity) Greek root of the word *asceticism*; part of the beliefs of the Pythagorean sect. He who does not succeed in keeping his body pure by following the rules of life also contaminates his soul.

Athenians residents of Athens who had civil rights and belonged to the *dēmos*. All free adult men of Athenian origin were citizens. Women, slaves, and immigrants had no civil rights.

Attic Delian Sea Alliance (477 BC) naval alliance, dominated by Athens, with the Greek cities in Asia Minor and the Aegean Islands, and the colonies in Thrace against Persia.

basileus (king) title of Greek rulers of small communities in the Dark Age.

boulē Council of 500 in Athens, comprising ten *phylae* (groups of fifty men each) annually selected to represent the entire city.

Bronze Age period in Greek history dating from ca. 2800 to ca. 1050 BC, characterized by the use of bronze weapons and tools. The Mycenaean and Minoan civilizations flourished during this period.

choregie Greek sponsors of theatrical productions and competitions.

chorus in Greek drama, the company of performers who explained and elaborated on the main action by singing, dancing, and narration.

Cleisthenes reformer who introduced democracy to Athens in 508–507 BC.

comedy originally, any play or literary composition with a nontragic ending.

Cynics from the Greek *kunikoi*. Followers of Diogenes and Antisthenes, they protested against the material interests of established society. Holding virtue to be the only good, they stressed independence from worldly needs and pleasures and led austere lives.

Cypselus seventh-century BC tyrant of the city of Corinth. His form of "affluence politics" was continued by Periander.

Darius king of Persia (521–485 BC); started the First Persian War. He annexed Thrace and Macedonia and undertook an expedition against Athens which ended in the Battle of Marathon.

Dark Age (ca. 1050–ca. 750 BC) period in Greek history so called because of the lack of information on it and because it formed an interim phase between the rich culture of the Bronze Age and the revival of culture in the Archaic Age.

Delphi city in central Greece, site of an Apollo sanctuary and an oracle. The utterances of Pythia, the priestess of the oracle, had great influence on personal and political life.

democracy from the Greek *dēmos* (people) and *kratein* (to rule); government by the people, either directly or through elected representatives. This form of government arose at the end of the sixth century BC in Athens.

Democritus (fifth century BC) Greek philosopher.

dēmos (people) originally a designation for the nonaristocratic part of the Athenian population. After the reforms of Cleisthenes, the word was used to designate all Athenians with civil rights.

Diogenes (ca. 400–325 BC) Greek philosopher and founder of Cynicism.

Dionysia Greek annual festival in honor of Dionysus, characterized by processions, poetry competitions, and theatrical performances.

Dionysus Greek god of wine, ecstasy, reproduction, life force, and of chaos and death.

dodeca polis twelve cities in Ionia.

Dorians Greek tribe that conquered parts of the Peloponnisos and Crete between 1200 and 1000 BC.

Doric Greek dialect spoken along the west side of Greece by the Dorians.

Draco Athenian statesman and lawgiver in the seventh century BC; drew up a harsh code of laws in 621 BC (Draconian Laws).

ecclesia the tribal meeting of Athens open to all citizens that, after Cleisthenes's reforms, made the final political decisions on internal and foreign affairs.

elegy from *elegos* (lament); a poem of lament and praise for the dead.

elektron alloy of gold and silver used in

the first coins minted in the seventh century BC.

Eleusis city on the Greek coast near Athens where mysteries were held between ca. 600 and ca. 400 BC.

emporion early Greek trading post dependent on its founding metropolis.

ephors college of five magistrates elected annually from the general meeting *(apella)*, forming the highest administrative and judicial authority in Sparta.

eupatridae Athenian nobles whose rule between 683 and 621 BC was ended by Draco.

Évvoia an island in the Aegean Sea.

gamiko special vases made for weddings.

gerousia council of elders in Sparta, consisting of twenty-eight men aged sixty and above, who were appointed for life.

Hades god of the underworld and brother of Zeus; also the name of the underworld itself.

harmonia harmony produced by the movement of the heavenly bodies.

Hector Trojan hero killed by Achilles in a duel during the Trojan War.

Hellen the legendary ancestor of the Hellenes, or Greeks.

helots members of the original population of Laconia and Messenia in Greece, subjugated and enslaved by the Spartans.

Hera wife and sister of Zeus, goddess of birth and marriage.

Heraclitus (ca. 500 BC) Ionian natural philosopher.

Hermes Greek god of travelers, shepherds, trade, and cunning. The son of Zeus and messenger of the gods, he also guided souls to the underworld.

Herodotus (ca. 484–424 BC) from Halicarnassus; father of Greek historiography; historian whose work *History* viewed the centuries-long battle between the Greeks and the Persians as a confrontation between Eastern and Western cultures.

hero brave mortal, often deified by the Greeks.

Hesiodus (ca. 700 BC) epic poet from Boeotia. He wrote the didactic poems *Thegonia*, on religion and mythology, and *Works and Days*, a sort of manual for farmers.

hippeis (horsemen or knights) dominant social class in Athens, comprised aristocrats with large landholdings who were rich enough to own a horse.

Hippias (reigned 528–510 BC) son of Peisistratus; Athenian ruler with his brother Hipparchus until 514 BC, then alone until forced out; last Athenian tyrant.

Homer (ca. 800 BC) legendary Greek poet to whom the epics the *Iliad* and the *Odyssey* are attributed.

homosexuality a sexual relationship between members of the same sex, acceptable in Greek society.

hoplites soldiers in the Greek heavy infantry, armed with sword, lance, and the large, round shield called the *hoplon*.

hoplon large round shield first carried by Greek heavy infantry in the Archaic period.

hydria a water jar.

hubris excessive pride.

iambic verse a poetic style with a short (or unstressed syllable) followed by a long (or stressed) syllable.

Iliad Greek epic poem attributed to Homer.

Ionian Rebellion (499–495 BC) rebellion of the Ionian coastal cities in Asia Minor and the neighboring islands against Persia.

Ionian natural philosophers philosophers of the sixth and fifth centuries BC who attempted to explain the cosmos through reference to nature and rationality, without recourse to mythology or religion. The first was Thales of Miletus.

Ionians Greek tribe driven from the mainland (except Attica) by the Dorians; settled on the Greek islands and on the west coast of Asia Minor in the ninth century.

Ionic Greek dialect of the Ionians spoken in Attica and Évvoia, on the Greek islands of Chios and Samos, and in the central part of the west coast of Asia Minor.

kalpis water pitcher.

kantharos vessel.

kernos ring-shaped vase.

kouros statue of a young man.

krater vessel in which water and wine are mixed.

krypteia random murder of *helots* (indigenous people made serfs) by young Spartans, possibly to prove their manhood. It intimidated the helots and reduced the risk of rebellion.

kurieia (guardianship) especially the guardianship over women, considered inferior, by an adult male representative.

kylix cup.

kypsel a chest.

Laconia the valley of the Eurotas River on the Peloponnisos Peninsula of Greece; original home territory of Sparta.

lekythos oil flask.

Leonidas (d. 480 BC) Spartan king who died in the Battle of Thermopylae with hundreds of Spartans, covering the retreat of the main Greek army from the Persians.

Leukippus fifth-century BC Greek philosopher and student of Parmenides. He laid the foundation for atomic theory with his hypothesis that "being" consisted of innumerable small particles which cause diversity in the world through their infinite combinations.

liturgy tax levy for rich Athenian citizens, consisting of a large sum spent on behalf of the state. This could involve financing the *gymnasium* (sports school) or a *choregie* (sponsors of theatrical productions), or equiping and commanding war ships.

Lycurgus ninth-century BC Spartan lawgiver and probable author of Spartan constitution.

lyric poetry originally written to be sung to the accompaniment of a lyre; one of two main types of poetry in ancient Greece. Lyric poetry was an independent genre but was also used in tragedies.

Magna Grecia region in southern Italy (sometimes including Sicily) where many important Greek colonies were situated, such as Thourioi, Crotone, Naples, and Tarentum (Taranto). The area was pervaded by a strong Greek influence.

Marathon city on the east coast of Attica, where the Persians suffered a devastating defeat in 490 BC by a small Athenian army under Miltiades.

medimner measure of wealth based on grain.

megaron a square building.

Messenia basin of the Pamisos River in southwest Peloponnisos conquered by Sparta in the seventh century.

metropolis mother city of a colony.

Mycale cape on the coast of Asia Minor, where the Persian fleet was defeated by the Greeks in 479 BC.

mysteries secret rituals said to liberate believers from earthly bonds.

nous eternal intelligence.

Odysseus Greek hero of the Trojan War.

Odyssey Greek epic poem ascribed to Homer, describing the journey of the Trojan War hero Odysseus to his home in Ithaca.

oinochoe wine pitcher.

oligarchy government by a small elite.

orchestra semicircular floor in theaters where actors originally performed and later, the chorus danced and sang.

Orientalizing period part of the Archaic period dating from about 750 to 650 BC when the Greek world was strongly influenced by the East with regard to religion, architecture, pottery, and the use of bronze and iron.

ostracism banishment; Greek citizens could vote to banish a political leader for ten years in order to prevent tyranny.

Pallas Athena Greek virginal goddess of wisdom, art and science, and handiwork, born from the head of Zeus.

Panathenaea great festival in Athens for Pallas Athena, goddess of the city, involving a procession to the Acropolis, where sports, music, and poetry competitions were held.

Parmenides fifth-century BC philosopher from Elea whose teachings contradicted the Ionian natural philosophy. The origin of the cosmos through the contraction of a proto-plasm and movement and change implied a vacuum, according to Parmenides. This was the "nonbeing" which could not exist. Only the unchangeable, absolute "being" existed. Origin and perishing were illusion.

Parthenon temple on the Athenian Acropolis dedicated to Pallas Athena, built between 447 and 438 BC.

Pausanias (d. 467 BC) Spartan general and regent for a Spartan king. In 479 BC, he was commander in chief of the Greeks at Plataea. He later conquered Byzantium and was condemned in 467 due to connections with the Persians.

pelikē type of amphora, a vase with handles.

Peisistratus (d. 528 BC) Athenian tyrant who assumed power first in 561 BC. He was driven away twice, but established his government in 546 BC.

pentakosiomedimnoi (five hundred medimners) highest social class in Athens, introduced by Solon and based on annual income expressed in terms of grain.

Periander (sixth century BC) son of Cypselus and tyrant of Corinth. He promoted the prosperity of Corinth by encouraging trade. According to Herodotus, his tyranny degenerated into a reign of terror.

Pericles (ca. 495–ca. 429 BC) the democratic leader of Athens in its Golden Age.

perioikoi (neighbors) original inhabitants living as freemen on the outskirts of the *polis* Sparta.

Persephone daughter of Demeter, the god-dess of agriculture; her recurring abduction by Hades and return from the underworld symbolize growth and decay of life.

Persian Wars wars between the Greek poleis and the Persians, instigated by the Greeks. The formal reason for the first war (492–490 BC) was the Greek support for the Ionian Rebellion. The second war (480–479 BC) marked the end of Persian power in the Aegean Sea.

phalanx a battle formation in the Greek infantry, usually consisting of eight rows of hoplites fighting in extremely close ranks.

Phoenicia kingdom on the west coast of Syria, a significant naval power after 1000 BC.

phylae ten divisions of the Athenian citizenry chosen as part of the 510 BC reforms of Cleisthenes. The ten *phylae* were each drawn from one urban, one coastal, and one rural district.

Plataea city in Boeotia where the Persians were defeated by the Greeks in the Second Persian War in 479 BC.

Pnyx hill in Athens where the tribal meeting, called the *ecclesia*, convened after the end of the sixth century BC. The hill was large enough to accommodate around 6,000 citizens.

polis autonomous Greek city-state.

Poseidon god of the sea, earthquakes, and volcanic phenomena, creator of the horse, brother of Zeus.

prytanes the fifty *boulē* (or Council of 500) members from one *phylae* who formed the daily administration of Athens for one-month periods.

Pythagoras (ca. 582–ca. 500 BC) Greek philosopher and mathematician, whose religious, political, and philosophical doctrines strongly influenced Plato. His work is known only from the philosophic sect he established in Crotone, the movement called Pythagoreanism, which believed in immortality and a concept of numerical mystery. It adopted an ascetic style of living.

Pythia priestess of the oracle at Delphi. She made her oracular utterances while in a trance; priests translated them into under-standable language.

pyxis round, earthenware box.

rhetors orator-politicians in Athens. With their rhetorical gifts, they had great influence on Athenian politics.

Salamis island on the west coast of Attica where the Persian fleet, under Xerxes, was defeated by the Greeks in 480 BC.

Sappho (ca. 600 BC) poetess from Lésvos who ran a school for girls from the aristocracy. Her verses to them are generally regarded as erotic.

satyr play Greek dramatic work with a heroic mythological theme like the tragedies, but with a humorous tone and a chorus of satyrs. It formed the last part of a tetralogy and was thus always performed after three tragedies.

skēnē a raised platform, precursor of scenery.

skyphos a beaker.

Socrates (ca. 470–399 BC) the most famous Athenian philosopher, his ideas were passed down primarily through the writings of Plato. He stressed virtue as knowledge, believing that if one knew the good, one would perform it rather than evil. Noted for his logic and style of questioning dialogue, he was condemned to death because of his alleged undermining of the democratic order.

Solon sixth-century BC Athenian law reformer who abolished debt slavery in 594 BC; expanded participation of all free citizens in government.

sophia Greek word for wisdom, or knowledge and insight.

Sophists Athenian teachers in the fifth century BC who gave popularized (and eventually denounced) instruction in philosophy, political science, rhetoric, and literature.

Sophocles (496–406 BC) famous Greek tragedian. Only seven of his works have survived: *Ajax, Antigone, Electra, Oedipus Rex, Trachinea, Philoctetus,* and *Oedipus in Colonos.* (There is also a large part of a satyr play he wrote, called the *Sleuth Hounds*.) He introduced the third actor in drama.

Sparta Dorian city-state in Laconia in the southern Peloponnisos.

Spartan upbringing education based on the austere lifestyle of Sparta; individuals were of secondary importance to the state and its army.

stoa sheltered promenade.

strategist one of ten commanders in chief in Athens, elected annually by the tribal meeting on the basis of his qualities.

symposium drinking feast.

Telestrion mystery temple, initiation building.

tetralogy four-part Greek play consisting of three tragedies and a satyr play.

Thales of Miletus (ca. 625–ca. 546 BC) Ionian founder of Greek philosophy.

Themistocles (ca. 525–ca. 460 BC) Athenian statesman who evacuated Athens in 480 BC; led the fleet in the Battle of Salamis.

Thermopylae mountain pass between

Thessaly and central Greece where Leonidas and hundreds of Spartans died covering the retreat of the Greek army from the Persians in 480 BC.

thetes social class in Athens, comprising small farmers and day laborers.

tholos a round building.

Thourioi colony founded by Athens in southern Italy in 443 BC, intended as a cultural model by Pericles.

Thucydides (ca. 445–400 BC) Greek historian of the Peloponnesian War.

thyrsus a staff with a pine cone on top, usually carried by the bacchants.

timocracy according to Aristotle, a state in which political power is in direct proportion to property ownership.

tragedy dramatic work originating from choral songs at the Dionysia festivals in Greece. Most tragedies had a mythological subject. They consisted of dramatic scenes with a maximum of three actors and the choir, alternated with choral songs.

Trojan War legendary war between Greek princes and Troy, provoked by the abduction of the Greek queen Helen.

Troy legendary city in Asia Minor near the entrance to the Dardanelles, besieged and destroyed by the Greeks during the Trojan War. Its ruins were discovered through the archaeological work of Heinrich Schleimann in the nineteenth century AD.

tyranny government seized unjustly by an absolute ruler. Between 650 and 500 BC in Greece, tyrants (absolute rulers) were often benign, receiving popular support.

vase painting style of earthenware decoration in the period following the Bronze Age. Attican black-patterned pottery of the sixth century was replaced by red-patterned pottery about 525 BC. The art of vase painting disappeared in the third century BC.

wanax lord.

Xenophanes (580–480 BC) itinerant Ionian philosopher and poet.

Xerxes I king of Persia (485–465 BC); destroyed Athens in 480 BC during the Second Persian War.

Zenon of Elea (fifth century BC) Greek philosopher and student of Parmenides.

zeugitai social class of economically independent farmers in Athens; owners of *zeugos* (yoke of oxen). The zeugitai served as foot soldiers in the army and, after Solon's reforms, could hold minor political offices.

Zeus supreme deity of the Greek gods.

Bibliography

The *Iliad* and the *Odyssey*

Heubeck, A. *Die homerische Frage: Ein Bericht über die Forschung der letzten Jahrzehnte.* 2nd ed. Darmstadt, 1988.

Kirk, G. S. *Homer and the Oral Tradition.* Cambridge, 1976.

McDonald, W. A., and Thomas, C. G. *Progress into the Past: The Rediscovery of Mycenaean Civilization.* 2nd ed. Bloomington, 1990.

Naerebout, F. G. "Male-Female Relationships in the Homeric Epics," *Sexual Asymmetry: Studies in Ancient Society,* J. H. Blok and P. Mason, eds., pp. 109-146. Amsterdam, 1987.

Patzek, B. *Homer und Mykene: mündliche Dichtung und Geschichtsschreibung.* München, 1992.

Siebler, M. *Troia-Homer-Schliemann: Mythos und Wahrheit.* Mainz, 1990.

Ulf, C. *Die homerische Gesellschaft: Materialien zur analytischen Beschreibung und historischen Lokalisierung.* Vestigia Bd. 43. München, 1990.

Wace, A. J. B., and Stubbings, F. H., eds. *A Companion to Homer.* London, 1963.

Crisis and Renaissance

Haegg, R., ed. *The Greek Renaissance of the Eighth Century BC: Tradition and Innovation.* Stockholm, 1983.

Jefferey, L. H. *Archaic Greece: The City-states c. 700-500 BC.* London, 1976.

Murray, O. *Early Greece.* Fontana History of the Ancient World. Glasgow, 1983.

Snodgrass, A. M. *The Dark Age.* London, 1971.

———. *Archaic Greece: The Age of Experiment.* London, 1980.

The Greek Expansion

Boardman, J. *The Greeks Overseas: Their Early Colonies and Trade.* London, 1980.

Dover, K. J. *Greek Homosexuality.* New York, 1980.

Fränkel, H. *Early Greek Poetry and Philosophy.* New York, London, 1973.

Graham, A. J. *Colony and Mother City in Ancient Greece.* Manchester, 1964.

Lesky, A. *A History of Greek Literature.* New York, 1966.

Malkin I. *Religion and Colonization in Ancient Greece.* Leiden, 1987.

Mosse, C. *La colonisation dans l'antiquité.* Paris, 1970.

Ridgway, D. *The First Western Greeks.* Cambridge, 1992.

Sparta and Athens

Cartledge, P. *Sparta and Lakonia: A Regional History, 1300–362 B.C.* London, 1979.

Clauss, M. *Sparta: Eine Einführung in seine Geschichte und Zivilisation.* München, 1983.

Hignett, C. *A History of the Athenian Constitution to the End of the Fifth Century B.C.* Oxford, 1952.

Link, S. *Der Kosmos Sparta: Recht und Sitte in klassischer Zeit.* Darmstadt, 1994.

MacDowell, D. M. *Spartan Law.* Scottish Classical Studies 1. Edinburgh, 1986.

Powell, A., ed. *Classical Sparta: Techniques Behind Her Success.* London, 1989.

Stockton, D. *The Classical Athenian Democracy.* Oxford, 1990.

Welwei, K.-W. *Athen: Vom neolitischer Siedlungsplatz zur archaischen Grosspolis.* Darmstadt, 1992.

The Greek Tyrants

Austin, M., and Vidal-Naquet, P. *Economic and Social History of Ancient Greece: An Introduction.* London, 1977.

Berve, H. *Die Tyrannis bei den Griechen.* München, 1967.

Finley, M. I. *The Ancient Economy.* London, 1985.

Kloft, H. *Die Wirtschaft der griechisch-römischen Welt. Eine Einführung.* Darmstadt, 1992.

Salmon, J. B. *Wealthy Corinth: A History of the City to 338 BC.* Oxford, 1984.

Stahl, M. *Aristokraten und Tyrannen im archaischen Athen.* Stuttgart, 1987.

Starr, C. G. *The Economic and Social Growth of Early Greece, 800-500 BC.* New York, 1977.

Greek Religion and Philosophy

Burkert, W. *Greek Religion: Archaic and Classical.* London, 1985.

———. *Orientalizing Revolution: Near Eastern Influence on Greek Culture in the Early Archaic Age.* Cambridge, MA, 1993.

———. *Ancient Mystery Cults.* Carl Newell Jackson Lectures, 1982. Cambridge, MA, 1987.

Burnet, J. *Greek Philosophy: Thales to Plato.* London, 1968.

Easterling, P. E., and Muir, J. V., eds. *Greek Religion and Society.* Cambridge, 1985.

Geyer, C.-F. *Einführung in die Philosophie der Antike.* Darmstadt, 1992.

Graf, F. *Greek Mythology.* München, 1987.

Guthrie, W. K. C. *A History of Greek Philosophy.* Cambridge, 1962-1981.

Kirk, G. S., and Raven, J. E. *The Presocratic Philosophers.* Cambridge, 1960.

Mylonas, G. E. *Eleusis and the Eleusinian Mysteries.* Princeton, 1961.

Parke, H. W. *Greek Oracles.* London, 1967.

West, M. *Early Greek Philosophy and the Orient.* Oxford, 1971.

Cleisthenes

Bleicken, J. *Die Athenische Demokratie.* Paderborn, 1994.

Farrar, C. *The Origins of Democratic Thinking: The Invention of Politics in Classical Athens.* Cambridge, 1988.

Jones, A. H. M. *Athenian Democracy.* Oxford, 1957.

Stockton, D. *The Classical Athenian Democracy.* Oxford, 1990.

Welwei, K.-W. *Die griechische Polis: Verfassung und Gesellschaft in archaischer und klassischer Zeit.* Stuttgart, 1983.

The Persian Wars
Bengtson, H., ed. *Die Mittelmeerwelt im Altertum 1: Griechen und Perser.* Frankfurt am Main, 1965.
Burn, A. R. *Persia and the Greeks: The Defense of the West 546-478 BC.* London, 1962.
Cook, J. M. *The Persian Empire.* London, 1983.
Walser, G. *Hellas und Iran: Studien zu den griechisch-persischen Beziehungen vor Alexander.* Darmstadt, 1984.

The Age of Pericles
Connor, W. R. *The New Politicians of Fifth Century Athens.* Princeton, 1971.
Connor, W. R. et al. *Aspects of Athenian Democracy.* Copenhagen, 1990.
Davies, J. K. *Democracy and Classical Greece.* Glasgow, 1978.
Meiggs, R. *The Athenian Empire.* Oxford, 1972.
Osborne, R. *Demos: The Discovery of Classical Athens.* London, 1984.
Schubert, C. *Perikles.* Darmstadt, 1994.

Greek Theater
Blume, H.-D. *Einführung in das antike Theaterwesen.* Darmstadt, 1978.
Else, G. F. *The Origin and Early Form of Greek Tragedy.* Cambridge, MA, 1967.
Herington, J. *Poetry into Drama: Early Tragedy and the Greek Poetic Tradition.* Berkeley, 1985.
Pickard-Cambridge, A. W. *Dithyramb, Tragedy and Comedy.* 2nd rev. ed. by T. B. L. Webster. Oxford, 1966.
———. *The Dramatic Festivals of Athens.* 2nd rev. ed. by J. Gould and D. M. Lewis. Oxford, 1988.
Stoessl, F. *Die Vorgeschichte des griechischen Theaters.* Darmstadt, 1987.
Winkler, John J., and Zeitlin, Froma I., eds. *Nothing to Do with Dionysos? Athenian Drama in Its Social Context.* Princeton, 1990.

From Pythagoras to Diogenes
Guthrie, W. K. *A History of Greek Philosophy.* Cambridge, 1962-1981.
Kirk, G. S., Raven, J. E., and Schofield, M. *The Presocratic Philosophers: A Critical History with a Selection of Texts.* Cambridge, 1983.
Lloyd, G. E. M. *Early Greek Science: Thales to Aristotle.* London, 1970.
McKirahan, R. D. *Philosophy before Socrates: An Introduction with Texts and Commentary.* Indianapolis, 1994.
Vander Waerdt, P. A. *The Socratic Movement.* Ithaca, 1994.
Vlastos, G. *Socrates: Ironist and Moral Philosopher.* Ithaca, 1991.

Further Reading

Arnold, F. *Greece.* Chatham, NJ, 1992.
Burrell, R. *The Greeks.* San Diego, 1994.
Dictionary of Classical Mythology. New York, 1983.
Dineen, J. *The Greeks.* New York, 1992.
Evslin, B. *Gods and Monsters of Greek Myths.* New York, 1984.
Ganeri, A. *Ancient Greeks.* Danbury, CT, 1993.
Graves, R. *Greek Gods and Heroes.* New York, 1965.
Homer. *Odysseus and the Giants.* Mahwah, NJ, 1984.
Millard, A., and Peach, S. *The Greeks.* Tulsa, OK, 1990.
Nichols, R., and Nichol, S. *Greek Everyday Life.* White Plains, NY, 1978.
Nicholson, R. *Ancient Greece.* New York, 1992.
Pearson, A. *Ancient Greece.* New York, 1992.
Poulton, M. *Life in the Time of Pericles and the Ancient Greeks.* Chatham, NJ, 1992.
Sauvain, P. *Over Two Thousand Years Ago in Ancient Greece.* New York, 1992.

Illustration Credits

Index

Text is indicated in roman type; illustrations are indicated in italic type.

Text is indicated in roman type; illustrations are indicated in italic type.

Text is indicated in roman type; illustrations are indicated in italic type.